DRIFTWOOD PRESS

ISSUE 8.2

EDITORS

CREDITS

Independently published by *Driftwood Press*
in the United States of America.

Fonts: Satellite, Garamond, Cinzel, League Gothic,
& Merriweather.
Cover Image & Content Illustrations: Kelsey M. Evans
Cover Design: Sally Franckowiak
Magazine Design: James McNulty

Published in July 2021
ISSN Print: 2578-7195
ISSN Online: 2331-7132
ISBN-13: 978-1-949065-12-1

Please visit our website at www.driftwoodpress.net
or email us at editor@driftwoodpress.net.

Table of

Contents

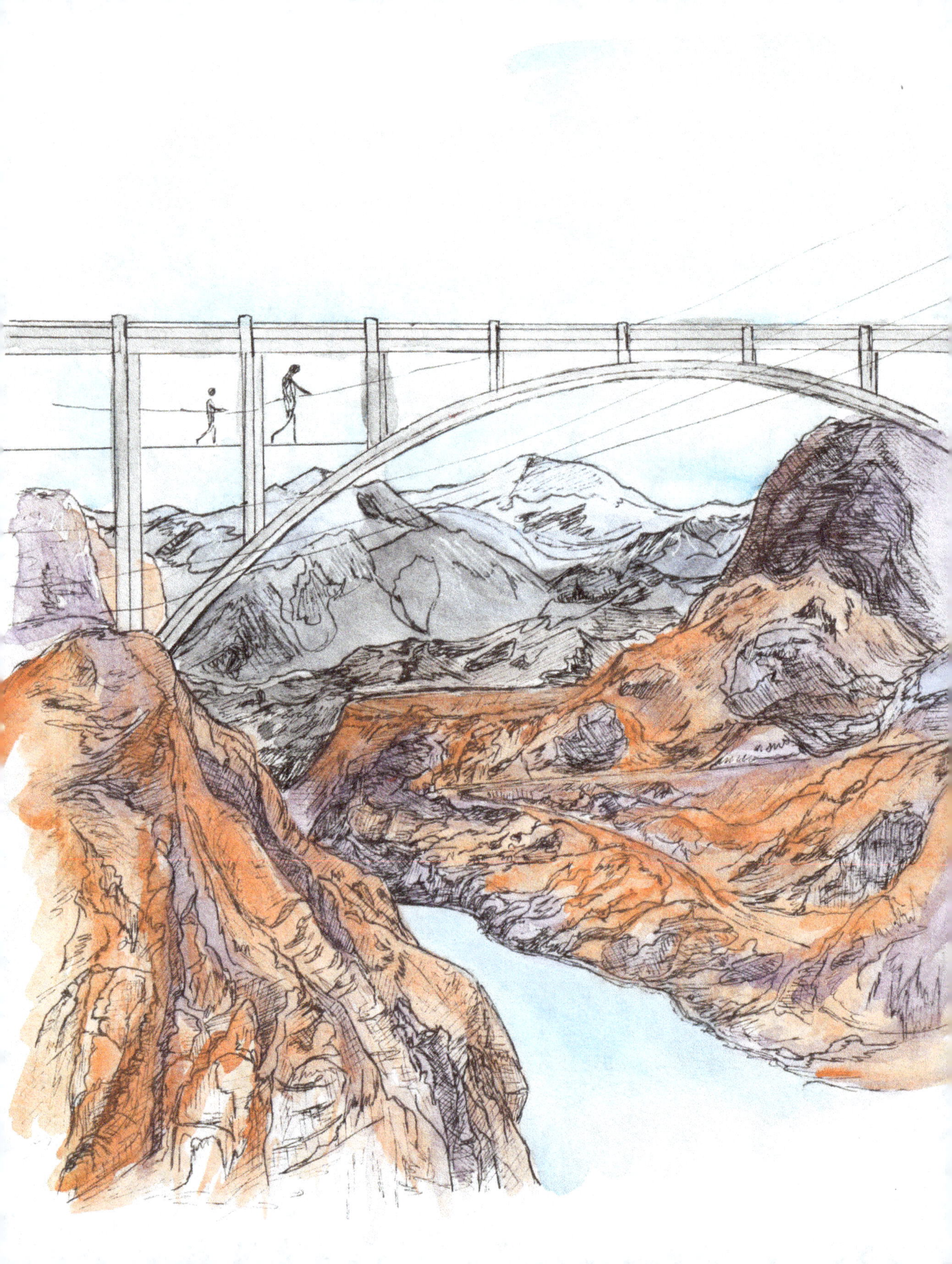

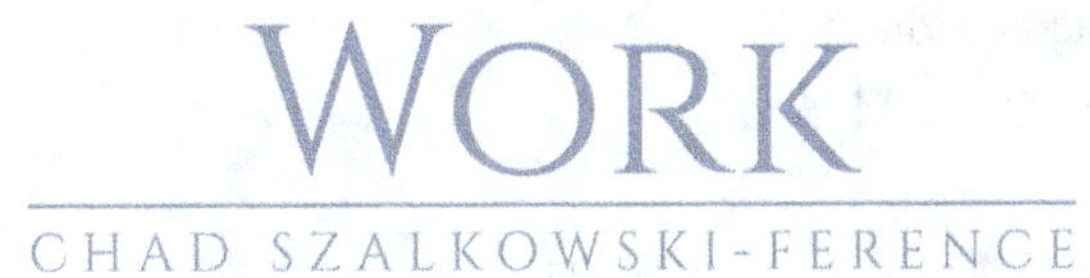

WORK

CHAD SZALKOWSKI-FERENCE

I

A blade the size and shape of a sperm whale edged alongside our Cobalt. I didn't notice the rig until it approached us on the right. In the future the blade would be attached to a shaft with two other blades to make a turbine. I noticed wind farms miles back—silver supplicants on the horizon positioned to receive winds drifting on the flats between mountains. Some spun. Others didn't. The ones that didn't frightened me. On the flat straight road I stared at the blade. I stared past my pregnant wife, Nova, in the passenger seat, convinced I'd see the yellow eye of the whale at the end of the blade. With my stare fixed, the car veered toward the flatbed, pulled gravitationally. Nova said my name. I'd been driving for hours. I righted the car.

She'd sat in the passenger seat with a pillow lengthwise against her torso. Keeping the nausea from spilling over preoccupied her. She didn't want the stomach acid to spew, numbing her teeth. She didn't want to retch, straining her viscera. Streams of clear saliva warned her constantly. Fourteen weeks pregnant, she'd been so alienated for so long from her body and self that she lived in this liminal space without remembering a before, with no expectation of an after. She lived to wait.

With the tractor-trailer in front of us, I got in the right lane. I stared at the agricultural sea of cabbage or strawberries or whatever type of greenery that grew there, ankle high in the vastness that spanned however many acres toward distant black mountains. I saw Silverados parked on the gravel road paralleling the expressway. Short white guys gathered behind the bed of one, the third in a series of three. The white guys wore flannels tucked into stiff jeans bunched from belts to boots, their eyes scanning the horizon. They watched the workers working, noting the time of day and what crop was left to pull.

Out in the field people harvested in clusters, bands of them bending at the waist with sacks slung across their backs, picking whatever crop that was. Out there, in groups, they looked to be on skiffs, fishing. Or harpooning. I focused on one group, and with their movements blurred by the distance and the speed of the car they looked to be a nonmoving fixture of the field, a modern interpretation of Stonehenge, made not of boulders but of bodies, the bodies making possible the impossibility of the harvest, the abundance of the American supermarket: an American pyramid.

"Where are we sleeping tonight?" Nova asked.

"I have directions for a motel," I said. "Unless you're thinking of somewhere nicer. While we have money."

At the side of the road there was a steel cutout of a stereotypical Western rancher family, mid-wave welcoming travelers. This steel cutout was twelve feet high—Pa in a yellow button-down and blue jeans over boots, Ma in a flower-print dress with flounced lace reaching up her neck, son in a miniature Pa getup.

"We need to save," Nova said

The steel cutout family passed in an instant as if virtual, an inch thick and propped with poles at forty-five-degree angles.

"El Rey."

"What did you say?"

"The King," I said. "El Rey Motel."

"We need to get water, too," Nova said.

II

I walked back to the car from the motel and told Nova that the concierge said a room was sixty a night.

"For this?" she asked, looking around at the horseshoe of units, a parking pad in front of each. It was a single-story motel.

"Should we keep looking?" I asked.

She picked her nails. "I can't be in the car any longer."

"Find a campground?"

"We'll camp soon," Nova said, picking her nails more intensely.

The doorknob rattled as I worked the key in. I learned the trick of getting the key to engage the parts of the lock's cylinder, turning the key with the knob. I'd expected a magnetized keycard. The odor of stale cigarette smoke came out of the room. The bed was made with mismatched bedding, a marble-patterned comforter folded at the end. The lamp on one side of the bed was an elegant hourglass shape with enamel coating, the lamp on the other side a cheap clamp desk light with a neon tube. The box TV hung suspended from the ceiling in a corner, protected against theft in a wire cage. I sat on a foldout chair at a card table and began rubbing my eyes.

"Sixty a night," I said.

"So long as there aren't bedbugs." Nova pulled the bedding aside and lay down.

"Could be in the tent," I said, making the chair squeak.

"I feel awful," she said. Her back faced me. "Just let me have a bed tonight."

I didn't respond but squeaked the chair after a pause.

I opened the gallery on my phone and looked at the photos I'd taken and wrote in my small, unlined notebook about the day: the Steinbeck museum, expensive and underwhelming and empty of visitors; the Henry Miller Library, a bookstore with overpriced hardbacks, made for the idle rich to feel earthy while enjoying internationally recognized folk musicians, at a hundred fifty dollars a ticket. The decision to write about this trip—roaming the country with only what we saved, seeking to make a home to raise a child in a mountainous area with likeminded people on little money—made me fault-finding.

But earlier, when I'd voiced this disappointment, Nova challenged me: "What did you expect—they're just buildings?" She was right. I hadn't thought about the actual experience of it. "You fucking romantic," she'd said, something she called me regularly.

That evening I lay in bed reading while she tended the rupturing pregnancy acne on her cheeks and chin and forehead. Whiteheads formed and crumbled in the California drought. They were hormonal, a recent hallmark. I dozed, the book dropping.

"Wake up," she said. "I'm not sitting in this room alone."

"Put something on," I said, setting aside the novel.

The TV zapped on, static and dust surging in sound at the center of the screen before the picture pixelated. There was no Wi-Fi.

I dozed again, and she elbowed me, so I got out of bed and turned off the neon tube and looked out the window.

All that we owned we'd packed into the backseat of the Cobalt and a carrier we strapped to the roof. We had four-thousand dollars and no home or job prospects. We imagined we'd end up in Asheville, the mountains of western North Carolina, where we'd imagined the progressive bubble there still contained a reality lacking in the hippie-yuppie Oregon university town we'd left. We didn't want Baby traveling the festival circuit preaching that love was all the world needed—love and body paint.

Soon Nova dozed, a thing so rare in these weeks of insomnia that I didn't move, didn't switch the TV off, didn't switch her light off. She needed any sleep she could get. My feet felt cold and filmy, and I wished I'd showered. As I watched her, her broad cheek illuminated by the glow of the screen, I thought about the work of the womb and about the locust-alien-looking fetus we saw on the ultrasound the week before we'd left Oregon. I thought about the strangeness of arms and legs growing from buds cell by cell, the umbilical cord and all that flowed through it to the fetus, a channel through which her own bodily fluids—oceanic, amniotic—flowed.

A mechanical scraping noise came from outside the opened bathroom window. It didn't wake her but startled me.

I stared in the darkness beyond her, into the bathroom along the far wall. Nova struggled to get care in the first weeks of pregnancy. Hospitals and midwives wouldn't see her unless she signed papers to deliver exclusively with them, provided insurance information. They apologized when she told them she didn't have insurance, intended to move soon. A doula finally agreed to consult her, but when Nova described the severity of the nausea, the doula suggested ginger capsules. At this, Nova's defeat registered in a sudden but subtle tilt of her head. She thanked the doula, unable to hold back a crack in her voice, followed by a sharp inhalation that retracted the escaped emotion. "I'll try the ginger," she said, with a smile I recognized as the one she gives when there's nothing left to be said, despite the misunderstanding.

In bed I eased on my side, slid my arm under my pillow and hers, and tucked the blanket partly between my legs. Like the doula, I felt indicted by the looks she gave that said what she didn't have to: I couldn't know. I tensed at the sound of a car pulling up, the noise of a man and woman getting out, going into another room. And I dozed. And then I dreamed the dream that I always have when I fall asleep anxious: the endlessly falling dream. But this iteration was different: as I fell I looked up not to the usual underside of a bridge under construction—four beams against an overcast sky—but to ribs and tendons and systems of viscera encased pink flesh, living flesh. The bodily cavity through which I fell, despite the functioning organs, was vast and airy.

We left before sunrise.

Hours later, the pumpjacks looked like deranged prehistoric birds lowering beaks to drink at dried-out streams as the counterweights and horse heads on either side of the I-beam rose and fell. This was the land of oil and roses, the top two commodities the county produced, Kern County. We passed through the flat heat of Bakersfield. Nova's green tea was still full in the cupholder. I looked out at the scrubland trying to visualize the oilfield below. It seemed impossible that it existed, that the pumpjacks had purpose.

In Vegas, at the hotel with the cheapest rates that night, Treasure Island, Nova waited on one of the couches along the wall while I waited in line to get a room. I felt the woven fabric that linked gold-plated stanchions. The others waiting for rooms snaked in a line that crisscrossed the lobby. I looked at them and recognized the collective delusions that kept my dad drinking, talking alone to the barmaid while imagining an audience, imagining memories. Ignoring the markers of despair that reflected in the mirror opposite the stool he straddled. I recognized the glee in some of their eyes. It was the glee I saw when my mom took me to open houses when I was young, homes priced at a quarter of a million dollars. The glee of eternal paradise. Standing in line I thought about my parents, who no longer spoke, their relationship centered on mutual animosity, not the emotional bond I thought a child could make. Standing there, I thought of the quote I saw yesterday on the wall of the Steinbeck museum, from Roland Wright, paraphrasing the writer's work: socialism will never come to America because we all see ourselves as millionaires, just temporarily embarrassed at the moment.

III

When I was a child I walked across a bridge under construction with my dad. We walked one foot in front of the other on a beam, a fall from which would have killed us. "Hold this," he said, grabbing a cable that paralleled the beam, which workers would clip harnesses to. I don't remember why we were walking, or where, and I didn't realize the intensity of it until I was older. I began having very specific falling dreams and began playing games with myself obsessively where if I walked off a crack or curb or grout line I would die, and then I remembered the stuttered step I took halfway across that beam. The beam notched an inch upward and I skimmed it mid-stride and took two halting steps with the same foot, gripping the cable. I paused, looked below at the debris around the narrow, gravelly creek—shopping carts, tires, a fridge, blue plastic bags, half buried or caught in twigs. I felt the presence of my dad surround me. He didn't touch me because he must have known that his touch would have caused me to overcorrect and topple into a freefall. "Take another step, one after the other," he said instead, in a strained way. And we walked on, and years later I asked what he'd have done if I'd fallen. "Jump," he said. Then he lightened the mood: "I couldn't face your mother." I wanted to ask—but didn't—what he thought I'd have done had he fallen.

We approached the Pat Tillman Memorial Bridge, which spans the Colorado River downstream from the Hoover Dam. The bridge is dedicated to an NFL safety who joined the military after 9/11, became one of the first soldiers to invade Iraq, and later died in eastern Afghanistan by American gunfire. As we crossed I thought about the people who jumped from the pedestrian walkway. I thought about the workers who must have died constructing the dam, the massive concave wall holding back the enormous waters of Lake Meade.

"How many people do you think died here?" I asked. "Building the dam and jumping?"

"Not as many as died in the wars Tillman fought," Nova said, eyes alert now because the landscape demanded we look.

"The dam looks like a headstone to me," I said.

"Looks like a uterus to me."

Transmission towers clustered around the dam. They seemed to grip the crags of the terrain, carrying hydroelectricity like neurotransmitters across synapses.

"It's a delicate balance," I said, restarting the conversation after it stalled.

"What is a delicate balance?" She closed her eyes again.

"Raising a child."

"I'll take that over what I have to balance now."

"I want Baby to have experiences—memorable experiences. But I also think I might be a sheltering parent."

There was no traffic, and I'd been keeping the driver-side tires on the yellow line, as if it were a crack.

"I had a conventional childhood, and it was memorable," she said. "Why are you in the middle of the road?"

"I imagine we'll be broke," I said. "Why wouldn't we be?" I moved back to my lane. "We'll just be working jobs and parenting."

She closed her eyes. After a while she said, "You're mad."

I asked what she meant. I didn't look over.

"You wanted to write about this trip. Camp." I heard her picking at her nails. "You're mad that I'm in this state."

"I'm not mad."

"You think it isn't as bad as I say."

"I know it is," I said. "You wanted this trip more than I did, so I'm sorry."

"You agreed to leave Oregon." I sensed she looked at me. "It's not like I needed to persuade you," she said.

"I wanted to go. This isn't about leaving Oregon." I looked so straight my vision blurred. The yellow line pulled me.

"What's it about then?" she asked.

"What—you started this discussion," I said, in a voice higher than I wanted.

"You've been brooding since—"

"Since when?"

"Since I've been sick," she said. "You were either at work or at the reservoir before we left."

"You couldn't get out of bed. You said I should get out while I still could before we left."

"It's not that," she said. I sensed she turned her head to look out of her window and then straight again. "You're in the middle of the road—God!"

"What is it then?" I waited a few moments before correcting my driving.

"You know."

"I don't."

"The way you told everybody," she said. Then she imitated me: "'Well, we ended our lease before she got pregnant, so I guess we still have to go.'"

"That's true," I said, looking at her.

"'Before she got pregnant'!"

I went quiet, looked ahead at the black pavement against the red desert, counted the passing transmission towers, the hanging conductors like massive cocoons.

"We got pregnant," she said into my silence. "We agreed to try."

"We thought it would take a long time," I said.

"And it didn't. And here we are."

"Here we are."

"I'm not going to apologize that we're not at some natural hot springs with naked, nonpregnant people."

"I'm fine. I'm driving. Plenty to write about."

"This is life," she said, more animated than she'd been in weeks. "I'm growing somebody inside me."

"This is life," I repeated. "I know."

IV

At work, before we left Oregon, I was kneeling on the cold concrete putting gallons of milk on rear-loading shelves when another worker named Cody walked into the cooler.

I worked the dairy shift, six in the morning until two. Cody stocked dry goods but kept his things in a box in the cooler—extra aprons and boxcutters and snacks from spoilage.

I turned to him and said that Nova told me what happened earlier in the shift. He'd ducked into the produce prep room where she was coring pineapples because he'd seen people from high school and didn't want them to see him, in his thirties, six foot three, a strawberry nametag, apron strings pulling on his neck.

"But it's necessary work," I told him in the cooler. "I'm not from here, so I don't have to worry about running into people. But I always tell myself it's necessary work, like the harvest."

He laughed it off. He had a way of being personable but never really present. "I just didn't feel like talking."

I continued: "And it's hard work. Down-stacking pallets, hefting fifty-unit egg cases, sliding columns of milk crates—few people today are burning those calories at work."

"Maybe," he said, "but this ten-dollar, sixteen-ounce unpasteurized superfood smoothie isn't necessary." He turned the product toward him. "'Reduces inflammation, reverses aging, revitalizes you,'" he read from the label, pointing at me.

I laughed, saying, "Well," and broke-down a box and moved a stack of flattened cardboard to a U-boat to take to the bailer. When I turned back to Cody, he'd already left the cooler. He'd taken his box of belongings with him.

That night, Cody committed suicide, hanging himself from a rafter in his parents' garage. During the next shift we all said we never would've thought he'd be someone to do that. "I can't believe it," everybody said, half the staff crying. I didn't mention that he'd removed all traces of himself from the cooler. I didn't mention our last conversation; I didn't think it was the cause, although the alienating nature of the work might have contributed to a larger alienation from self. Nova vomited for the first time, mistaking the work of surging pregnancy hormones for the disorienting effect of grief.

V

We drove into whiteness. Out of habit I engaged the wipers and they streaked across the dry windshield. It looked like snow blanketed the desert a millennia ago and never melted, could never melt. The sky now overcast, the woolen gray of the clouds blended with the sand—the dust of gypsum—of this flat stretch, and I felt I'd driven into a snow squall, and with the loss of anything to contrast the degrees of whiteness I became disoriented and needed to pull over. I studied the road, and as gusts shifted the sand I was able to make out the yellow dividing line. I decided to drive in the middle of the road, eyes fixed on that line when it appeared.

"Where are we?" she asked when she awoke.

"Tularosa Basin," I said. "White Sands National Park."

She sipped water, waited to see if that water would stay down. "Hurts my eyes—in every direction nowhere to look."

"I am sorry," I said and endured the quiet that followed.

"It would be pretty if it weren't terrifying," she said as I was about to repeat myself.

"How could I never know this existed," I said instead of repeating my apology, not knowing whether we'd keep to ourselves our thoughts of the last hour.

"It's America," she said, looking out at it.

The road began to clear and I could distinguish lanes. Beyond the road, before the dunes, there were slight rises made of soft rounded bumps. I remembered the first time I thought the fetus expired. Nova lay on a padded table in what had been the dining room of a bungalow, now a naturopathic doctor's office. She agreed to meet the first time for free. I sat in a straight back chair along the wall. The ND asked Nova to unbutton her pants and pull them down lower, and she greased the soft rise of flesh of a belly that had yet to protrude much. The ND said that extreme nausea was a good sign because that meant that the hormone was strong, "protecting the little one, though we know it's no fun for Mama." Her practiced hand moved the wand around her navel, searching out a heartbeat. Time passed, and she greased again. I saw a tear gathering in the corner of Nova's eye. I felt indifferent to a miscarriage but didn't like imagining what it would be like to pass the ghost of something that never was. The ND expanded the radius of her search. Trebly pricks came from the speaker in the hand that didn't hold the wand. Nova looked down, chin on chest.

"That's Mama's," the ND said.

Nova's head fell back to the padded table, dislodging the tear.

"It is more than likely that the back is facing the navel. But since you did have the spotting, I'll write you a script for a vaginal ultrasound. I want to reassure you, though, that I'm not worried. It is just a little early to pick up a heartbeat on this machine."

I looked over at Nova now in the car as she rolled down her window. I slowed. She didn't vomit but expelled mouthfuls of saliva as they pooled around her tongue. I said I'm sorry again but with the flat tone I took whenever she threw up. "At least we know the heart still beats," I added.

"Baby will have no idea any of this happened," she said, indicating the sickness and surrounding whiteness.

We drove deeper into the interior of White Sands. Dunes now rose. I pulled over and we got out to walk up a dune to see the view. As I walked around the car and took in the moonscape, I imagined that we were the first to explore a city flattened by nuclear warheads, the whiteness all around us the bleached soot of burnt bones. I imagined we walked on a traceless people, the labor of living erased, and I walked up the dune mournfully, privately performing my daydream. She shaded her eyes from the diffuse sunlight that shone above, below, and peripherally. I didn't find it that bright, but she spent the majority of the day with her eyes closed, not sleeping. We reached the top and looked south where black craggy peaks separated the dunes from the overcast sky. It looked two-dimensional, not three, one feature of the landscape stacked on top of the other.

We heard children's voices and looked toward a dune across from where we parked. A brother and sister, carrying red and purple circular sleds, beating hearts on a backdrop bereft of color, scrambled to the top. Their parents stood beside the car, instructing them, scolding them. Nova grabbed my hand and held it, and this was so rare for us I felt the need to pull her close for a hug, my forearms finding familiar notches above her hips. Now we looked in opposite directions, she to the brother and sister sledding on sand, I to the west, out of where we'd driven.

She said, "Soon we'll take our kid sledding."

This was the first time either of us referred to the fetus, just entering the second trimester, as anything other than the article-less, capitalized Baby. The first time either of us referred to it in a specific, concrete way. This baby was coming. She would go into labor, push this person out into the world, and the hospital would expect us to walk out with it—I still couldn't conceptualize it—and strap it in a car seat and drive.

"Soon," I said.

We walked back down the dune, leaving dragging footprints in the white sand, and I had another daydream, this one also deeply depressing—a person with a nebulous face, in their forties, a person I knew to be our offspring, wearing khaki pants and a short-sleeved collared shirt, a uniform, saying in a bitter, gossipy tone, "I don't know what the dayshift does all day because they leave us all the work."

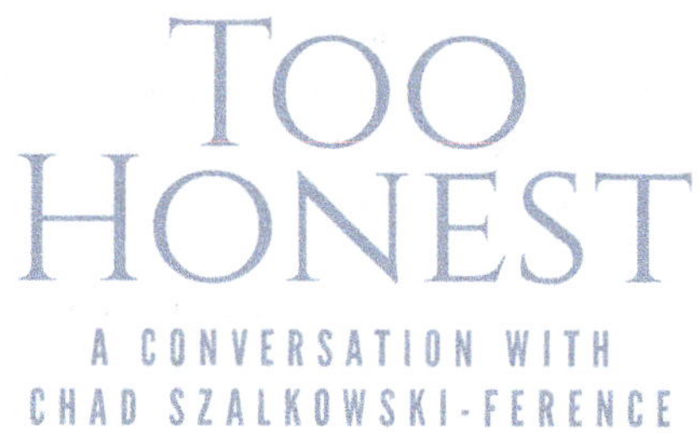

Too Honest

A Conversation with Chad Szalkowski-Ference

The following conversation was conducted by managing fiction editor James McNulty.

James McNulty: Hey, Chad! Congrats on wrapping up the long trek to publication! We're so excited to feature this layered story in our magazine! There's so much to talk about, and I'm excited to get started.

Chad Szalkowski-Ference: Hey, James! Thank you so much for selecting the story for publication—and especially for all the close readings and the shaping feedback you and your team of editors provided. The story is so much stronger now because of you all. I'm grateful for that. It was a long trek: it was both despairing and exciting!

JM: I'm glad to hear the long road paid off, but let's chat more thoroughly about how the revisions changed this piece a little later in the interview. I think the first thing I want to delve into is the role creative nonfiction played in this draft. You were trained in CNF, right? I think these roots come across pretty clearly in "Work," but how do you think they've influenced the piece?

CF: Sure, great question. I do have an MFA in creative nonfiction. I don't want to call it a phase, but my early writing days were very heavily involved with travel writing and long-form war reporting. I think it is clear how these genres (obsessions) show up in the story. It is a road narrative, and imagery of war appears throughout. Being someone who was in his late teens during 9/11 and its aftermath, someone into radical politics from that age on, I followed the wars closely and wrote about them on blogs (when people were on Blogger and WordPress) and other places.

And so when I applied to MFA programs, it seemed natural to choose the CNF track. In fact, much of this story directly grew out of my MFA thesis manuscript. When I entered the low-residency program, I really was living out of a car with my pregnant wife who was really suffering from extreme nausea. But when I say that I don't want to call my writing and reading of CNF a phase, I do think I hit a limit as to what I was able to produce in the genre. I wrote the manuscript and the program accepted it and I was awarded the degree, but then I couldn't improve it. I sent it off to some publishers who were calling for book-length place-based projects. I received one personal, detailed rejection letter. And when I sat down to reassess the thing, I realized I didn't really read any literary nonfiction anymore. I read fiction and drama mostly.

I decided to try to take a fresh look at themes I gravitate toward without feeling a need to be faithful to experience. It felt liberating to break out of the contract that CNF establishes with readers: to highlight and craft but not invent out of whole cloth. I felt I couldn't gloss details in CNF even if the reader didn't want or need them. For example, I also really walked across a bridge beam with my dad as a kid. But when I wrote about that experience *truthfully*, I couldn't help but say that it didn't really affect my life. I overexplained everything because I felt the need to level with readers (an urge I still have—as you know because you helped me eliminate some of those moments in this story). I couldn't let images speak for themselves, which I think (I hope) I'm able to do better in fiction.

But to answer your question more directly: the narrator in this story is a writer and writes to catalog. He also views what he catalogs with a political lens. He sets out to test a particular perspective of the world, and I think that comes out of the CNF I studied during my MFA days—books like Chris Offutt's *The Same River Twice* and Eula Biss's *Notes from No Man's Land.* Not to mention classics like Steinbeck's *Travels with Charlie* and Henry Miller's *The Air-Conditioned Nightmare.*

JM: Could you explain more fully what you mean by your want to "level with readers"?

CF: By leveling with readers, essentially, I mean providing *all* the details that I know as the person who experienced the thing about which I'm writing. It means being *too* honest, being unable to take creative license: I felt the urge even to alert the reader that the dialogue I was writing was an imperfect reconstruction, not verbatim. I would deflate other things as well, such as imagery and symbolism. CNF requires a balancing that I don't think exists in fiction, and I couldn't ever find the balance. Lee Gutkind, the founder and editor of *Creative Nonfiction*, describes the genre as "true stories, well told." It's a simple description, but I could never really stick the landing of artfully crafting a narrative that remained true to experience.

A perfect example of this type of writing is Jo Ann Beard's "The Fourth State of Matter," the wonderfully crafted and startling and tragic narrative of a mass shooting at the University of Iowa. Beard, who knew the shooter and those who were killed, is able to account for the intimate aspects of her life with well-placed details and dialogue, as well as capture so much thematic emotion in imagery—such as with wings trapped in amber, the plasma in Saturn's rings, the longevity of a life captured in prose.

I couldn't figure it out. This is not to say that CNF is more difficult to write than fiction; it's just that I think I am more comfortable writing fiction. I can write better without the readerly expectation that the prose approximates lived experience as closely as possible.

JM: So "Work" was always conceived of and written as fiction? I know you said it bloomed from your CNF thesis. Were parts of it directly taken from the thesis, or did you write "Work" from scratch as fiction with the thesis in mind?

CF: Yes, "Work" was definitely conceived of and written as fiction. My thesis mentor, Kristin Kovacic, would definitely recognize similar themes and locales, but when I sat down to write the story, I wrote away from what I wrote in the manuscript. I didn't look at it; if anything appears in the story that appeared in the manuscript, it crept in through memory. I found the writing came easier and truer when I approached it as imaginatively as possible—that is, without envisioning myself as narrator.

JM: Nonfiction is perhaps sometimes better than fiction at illustrating an entire worldview, something I think "Work" is successful in doing. We don't often publish stories with overt political leanings here at *Driftwood*, but "Work" seems the exception. Could you talk to me a little bit about the worldview and politics of "Work"?

CF: I'm glad this is the exception! My writing tends toward the political, something I'm trying to move away from. To be honest, I thought in the beginning of the process that the politics resonated with you as a person and moved the needle on your decision to work with me to get this story into the publishable column. And *so much* of the prose needed to be reworked. In a way, then, I think the politics both saved it and made it so difficult to edit and revise.

We have talked about democratic socialism in our many correspondences. There is a lot of that in here, but if I had to talk about the worldview and politics of this story, I would think in terms of anarcho-syndicalism. Without going into the depth about the nuances, I am thinking of an organic community dedicated to self-sufficiency, one that is democratic but also decentralized (unlike the centralized concentration of political power in Washington, DC, in our democratic, capitalist, imperialist country). I'm thinking of what Chomsky talks about when he talks about the libertarian left. In the story, there is tension between necessary work and work that feeds the commodification of everything, and there are many images of the necessities of human life—community, reproduction, housing, the harvest, the wind turbines, the oil fields, hydroelectricity, and so on. I think what the narrator and Nova are seeking out—impossibly—is an anarchist enclave where they can work and raise a child without the alienation that laboring in the service or gig economy or laboring to produce surplus value for capital holders entails.

I don't want to be long-winded here, but I want to mention something that Checkov said, something I've been thinking more and more about. He said the "solution of the problem" isn't what should concern the artist, but "the correct formulation of the problem." I'm not entirely sure if "Work" meets that standard, but I hope the ending gets at how difficult it is to escape the system of nationalism and capitalism.

JM: I can't speak for others, but I do think the story speaks well to the fatigue of producing only for commodification's sake. You're not wrong in my personal political resonation: I certainly appreciated the whole worldview compressed into this single story, and I tend to agree with much of what the story is putting forward in terms of its titular theme. But the writing community is by-and-large very liberal, so we get hundreds of stories with agreeable politics; that alone wouldn't really help put a story ahead here. At *Driftwood*, we're looking for sharp language more than anything, and your story—from the first page onward—*sings*. We did very little revisions to the argument scene, the opening, the father-son flashback, and the last section, which all came in pretty *finished*. But yeah, we worked with you a good bit on the surrounding areas—how to *show* your themes outside of narration, how to keep plot momentum without wandering into travel writing too much, how to tighten the story so that every paragraph contributed to the character or theme without re-covering something already shown, etc.

Part of where I was going with these nonfiction questions is that it's easy to see the influence of CNF on "Work"—particularly that of travel writing. Your earlier drafts, too, showed a lot of wandering, soaking up the landscape and the surrounding people—a lot of travel writing, which my editors and I argued needed pretty significant cutting to have the necessary momentum needed for short fiction. Do you want to walk readers through some of the cut scenes? I know you said the story is "so much stronger now" because of the on-going feedback we provided, but I'm sure you also had to cut some of your darlings—realizing that you liked moments that just weren't working for the overall story.

CF: I'm relieved the sharp language carried the day. One thing I pay close attention to—as a reader and writer—is the diction and rhythm of the sentence.

And you're right about the clashing of genres becoming an issue during revision. There was a lot of wandering and observing in the early drafts. I'm thinking of the long scene at the rest stop and a lot of the movement in the Vegas scene. In the travel writing that I've done and the more general creative nonfiction that I've done, I had a tendency to catalog things and images. And the narrator was doing that: looking out and stacking images and details, trying to get at the totality of the scene. Much of that, I think, could work in a longer piece, especially if readers sat down expecting that. But as you point out, the short story needs to be economical; each paragraph needs to forward characterization or plot or deepen or complicate themes in interesting, subtle ways. A lot of the cataloging in the earlier drafts were little more than reiterations of things already established.

In terms of darlings that I killed, there are a few. There are little things, like I described a thin man at a rest area as "thin as an orchid." I'm not even sure if that's good writing, but I like the phrasing and the image it elicits. I might have to work that into a later story. But that's minor. The more major cuts that still remain with me come from the greater milieu of Vegas, particularly the panhandlers and pawn shops, the strip malls and The Strip. Trump International Hotel. The characters walking through Treasure Island, taking in the smells, the patrons, the desperation. These scenes were difficult at first to cut. I spent portions of the night justifying them in my head. But they ultimately lost because when I removed them and placed them at the end of the document, I could see the major points of the story speaking more clearly to one another. Once they were gone, I felt unburdened. And energized.

There were also duds that I cut on your advice, such as the scene I added briefly about making coffee with a battery-powered kettle and the irrational customer in the dairy cooler scene in the second-to-last section. These I don't miss at all.

I'll say one more thing about revision: I always trust editors. I tend to do what they tell me, not because I want them to publish me but because I respect the position. I teach composition and stress that writing is social and that writing is not perfectible and that all writers have more to learn. I take that same energy to fiction. Everybody has an ego, and so being told that the thing you've created and are invested in is not quite good enough does sting. But writing is writing and the ego is the ego: they're not tied together, or at least shouldn't be. After the initial smack fades, I'm ready to work with others on the writing. And at *Driftwood*, you and your team of editors, I think, are unique. You all care about the writing and the process. I'm sure you know and I don't have to tell you, but many journals do very little with the writers they publish. You know, you get an acceptance and then a notification of when it comes out, and maybe they send you a couple copies, and that's it. *No writing happens.* And that depresses me. But at *Driftwood*, you and your editors worked with me closely and considerately, always making sure the story didn't drift too far from where I intended it to go, making sure I saw the value in the revisions, making sure the revisions were still the product of the creative process. The result is a strong story, strong literary magazine, and strong relationships.

JM: Sounds like we should hire you as our spokesman, had we the money. I'm glad the revision process worked out for you; it's been a long while since we had someone who hated the process, though I think everyone feels a little burnt on the first line edit—especially when they have no experience working with an editor at such an intense line-by-line level. As you said, most presses accept "as is" and move along with their day. I think horror stories of Dickinson's poetry and Gordon Lish taking creative control away from the writer have chased the idea of working intensely with editors out of fashion. I hear this is becoming a trend with some bigger presses, too; Colson Whitehead told one of my editors at an MFA lecture that his editors didn't ask for *any* revisions for *The Underground Railroad.* We value fiction, the craft, and the process too much to not work with the writers to improve their craft. But yeah, it's definitely a tightrope walk on the editors' side: you have to be as descriptive as possible, never—or rarely—veering into prescriptivism; you have to leave the final say in the author's hands; the feedback always needs to be measured for tone; you need to recognize what's asking *too much,* and if you do decide to ask for a lot (be it cutting full scenes, as we did, or restructuring), you need to be clear and honest with the writer about that and make sure they agree.

I think you're also right that the difference in genre (short story vs creative nonfiction) expectations and length was the primary focus of our revisions. And though there was strong language throughout, I don't mean to say that's the only thing that encouraged us to move forward with this piece; the scenes I mentioned before, which I'd like to chat about more thoroughly later, went through the process nearly untouched. I think I also noted to you in our emails that there was great emotional honesty throughout—potentially a beneficial carryover from CNF.

One thing that went through a bit of change during revisions but was relatively uncommented on by my team was your structure. Could you talk to me about why the story is broken into parts, and how those parts morphed over the course of revisions?

CF: I'll do the job for free! I am trying to get a full-time teaching job, trying to get out of the adjunct hustle, so I feel like a lot of the work I'm currently doing is just for a CV line—just to make myself appear more appealing on paper to future hiring committees.

Joking aside, the revision process was difficult, but that is what we are here for. I remember reading an interview with the fiction editor at *The New Yorker,* Deborah Treisman, and she said no writer escapes the editing process. I think I remember her mentioning that even writers such as Don DeLillo get suggestions. If DeLillo gets red ink, there's absolutely no reason for me to catch feelings about it.

Yes, the structure. I think the structure is another carryover from CNF, especially the travel writing subgenre. I wanted it to be a very place-based piece. I wanted the narrator's disposition and preoccupation to reflect the landscape and atmosphere. Each section is set in a different locale, and each locale (I hope) influences the tone and content of the story. On the road, I think, wandering, when we have no solid destination, when we've never seen what we're seeing, we tend to become more invested in our surroundings. The background typically becomes foreground. And it seems to me at least a largely private occurrence. Something each of us experiences differently because each of us has a different set of experiences that pings in our consciousness, that is called up due to what we see and hear and sense in the moment. I think that on the road and in the car—just two people—is a good place to explore that. And the narrator and Nova, except for a brief moment at the end, never really find a connection, despite the sameness of their surroundings.

As you say, much of the structure stayed the same. I played around with sections one and two because I wasn't, at first, quite seeing how differently the motel scene was from the initial stretch of driving that opens the story. It seems obvious now, but in the thick of writing, you get lost in your original plans: originally, what became section one was just supposed to be a quick little intro that got the characters to the motel. But the section kept growing and taking on thematic weight. It wasn't until our second or third round of revisions where it hit me to separate them.

Another reason is that I like to write what I like to read. And I like hard breaks in writing. Breaks that surprise the reader. As a reader, I like not being able to predict what the next sentence, the next section, the next chapter will feel like. I'm actually currently reading a perfect example of what I'm talking about: Carlos Fuentes's *The Crystal Frontier.* In that novel, at least so far, and I'm about halfway through, each chapter is told by a different character, from a different point of view, and in a different style. I find a certain magnetism and dynamism in that kind of writing, which I try to emulate in this story.

JM: You mentioned the lack of connection between Nova and the narrator. The argument scene in part three was one of the scenes that stayed relatively untouched from first to final draft. I think you nailed that scene from the get-go, and yet writing argument scenes are so tricky—particularly ones between spouses. It's easy to fall into melodrama whenever emotions are heightened, of course. What advice do you have for writers looking to write arguments? Why do you think this one works?

CF: One thing that I'll mention that did change in the argument scene, which I think will help answer this question, is that you suggested a little more character movement to show action between spurts of dialogue. In revisions, then, I had characters look a certain way, pick fingernails, or veer toward the other lane while driving. All good additions, no doubt. But when I set out to write this argument scene, I wanted it stripped down, pure back and forth. I looked at it as an exercise. So I set out to write the best dialogue I could, trying to have the dialogue alone carry the burden.

By that I mean, first, I followed Sol Stein's advice to give the characters different scripts. Each character exists in their own world with their own needs and preoccupations. Their speech should reflect that. This happens in real life, too. Often people carry on two or more conversations at once, talking past each other or pivoting abruptly. I think the characters do this—speak from their script. And, second, I make sure the script reveals character; that's important. To write a character, you really have to know that character. It's a crafted, artful thing. Dialogue is indirect characterization. When I read bad dialogue, I see how the writer hasn't connected it with characterization; it seems to me that bad dialogue comes from writers viewing it as separate from characterization and more meant primarily to provide exposition.

I think the argument scene works well because it follows those two rules of thumb. And it is restrained. So much is left unsaid. I think when characters start articulating the obvious is when the melodrama starts. It is especially bad when characters start providing exposition with heightened emotions: "This is just like last year when you cheated on me with your high school sweetheart you reconnected with on Facebook!"

I guess my advice would be to say that your characters, if they're full characters, should always have a number of things running through their heads at all times. You should know them that well. And their speech should be inflected with those things, and the story should be about those things. Story is about character—in revealing themselves, characters create action; they don't simply respond to it. And don't think fillers such as "like" or "um" or "ah" make dialogue realistic. Those things aren't realistic representations of speech, and even if they were, dialogue itself isn't meant to be realistic. It's meant to make art. Art can be realistic, but that's not its primary purpose.

And read drama. I learn a lot about writing from studying how playwrights, with basically just dialogue and stage directions, handle a handful of characters stuck together in a handful of places for two hours. At the beginning of this answer, I mentioned that you suggested more character action; when I wrote that action into the scene, I treated it like stage directions.

JM: I think your note about refraining from having characters articulate the obvious is perhaps most important here. Too often submissions feature argument scenes with exclamation marks sans the surprise—an almost oxymoronic move. When a character says what we're expecting, the argument often devolves into cliché and melodrama. Your characters' reactions and responses consistently surprise, and they *reveal* character more than *confirm* it.

We tend to promote the practice of balancing the four modes of writing (action, description, dialogue, and interiority) here at *Driftwood.* To best visualize and *feel* the world of the story, we don't think you can drop those exterior modes (action and description) for a significant length of time: if a writer lets interiority overwhelm, the narrative often fails to move forward and the world, setting, characters, and scene are impossible to visualize; if a writer lets dialogue overwhelm, the characters become floating, talking heads, impossible to visualize with no external setting or gestures to confirm or betray the truth of what they're saying. (I should note here that even techniques such as stream of consciousness feature exteriority, though it's *filtered through* the interior.) Featuring exteriority alongside the other two modes helps the world feel more believed, seen, and *felt.* Exteriority also helps the pacing of the story, among so many other things.

One of the most stunning moments in the story features a father and son in a perilous situation. Could you talk to me a little bit about the inspiration for this scene? The two-punch at the end is especially emotional: "And we walked on, and years later I asked what he'd have done if I'd fallen. 'Jump,' he said. Then he lightened the mood: 'I couldn't face your mother.' I wanted to ask—but didn't—what he thought I'd have done had he fallen."

CF: The inspiration for this scene is one of the great mysteries of my life. The action of the scene is from memory: my dad and I did exactly what is described here. My parents were good parents—I always felt loved—but they're a little more wild than the average person, and we were poor, and as a result I had a very different childhood than most. It was one reason I was initially drawn to CNF: I could write my own *The Glass Castle*! But when I say it is a mystery, I mean that all of the emotion and the hangups that the narrator has about this scene are not mine. I've never *felt* what the narrator feels, never, for example, tried obsessively not to step off cracks. Last year, my dad sent a picture from the bridge we walked over when it was just beams, and I just texted back something like, "haha, that was crazy," but I wonder if it sticks more with him. We talk about it on the surface only.

But the emotional inspiration for the scene comes from my now being a parent to a six-year-old. I've had all the nightmares parents have: children falling, drowning, going missing. And I have had a few that have really messed with me. So when I wrote this scene, I tried to live in this fear, in that ruined state.

About the last two lines you quote: I do think those are important, and maybe they come more from my own experience than I'm admitting. I think it shows a father more self-centered than one should be, which is probably the unstated rift that separates the narrator from his father and causes the parental anxiety more generally throughout the story.

JM: One of the later additions in revision was part four: the Cody backstory. Could you talk a little about "necessary work," essential workers, and what Cody's story adds to the themes of "Work"?

CF: The Cody backstory was definitely the most difficult to get to feel natural, to make poignant, to become an active scene. It took a lot of writing and rewriting and "thesis statements," as you suggested as an exercise. Whole iterations of the scene were discarded. And I still don't have it all the way worked out.

But what I wanted to highlight here is how even necessary work—bringing food to communities—becomes alienating because even foodstuff falls to commodity fetishism. So the unpasteurized superfood smoothie is no longer the product of the earth, the harvest, the production, the transportation, the stocking. Now, its value is purely a relationship with itself and the consumer, and it primarily provides status (not nutrition) in exchange for money. The collection of workers that make that commodity gets erased, in the mind of the consumer, and the collection of workers has no connection to the product either.

The Cody backstory provides a backdrop or a foreshadowing of the potential future for the child Nova carries: even the child, the product of the most essential *labor*, becomes alienated, finds no value or purpose (beyond the biweekly paycheck) or community in the work they do.

JM: I think that message comes through very clearly in the final lines especially, though of course more emotionally conveyed than intellectually (the benefit of fiction over essays, I'd argue).

The thesis statement exercise isn't one I use too often, but your story was pretty thematically focused—even the title implies a socio-political message. These types of stories can often benefit from this exercise—the writer creating a thesis statement for their own personal use, then holding that thesis statement up to the story to make sure it's reflected in each scene. The danger of this exercise, of course, is that the thesis statement might somehow make it *into* the story, rather than existing solely for the writer's use. We never had that issue with your story, but I can see that being a possible pitfall to this practice—the story becoming too academic and heavy-handed if the writer takes the exercise too far.

Besides CNF, what other mediums have influenced your work? How?

CF: We've talked about film, and that is a medium I've learned from. For example, you recommended I watch *First Reformed* because much of it aligned with the themes of "Work." And from that film, I learned (or relearned—I need reminders of the basics regularly) how to pace, how to make flashbacks tight and revealing, how fully backstories need to be worked out (even if they aren't directly *shown*), how do deal with contemporary politics artfully, and so on. I like genres, as we've been discussing, that can be experienced in a single sitting, where we can get the totality at once, more or less. Film, drama, and the short story provide that. And I've recently been consuming a whole lot of these genres, paying special attention to what they *don't do,* how much each trusts the audience to make connections, to make meaning. I've been learning to be more sparse, more suggestive.

JM: I'm glad you enjoyed *First Reformed.* I happened to see that for the first time a few months before reading this submission, and I saw some kinship there. Talk to me about other specific filmmakers or writers who have influenced your writing. Do you think of yourself as belonging to any particular tradition? If so, who are your masters and who are your contemporaries?

CF: This is a question I've always wanted to answer, but now that I've been asked, I'm nervous to name authors, worried I'll seem pretentious or seem to be placing myself way above my station. But writers that made me love reading and made me want to try writing are very different: Virginia Woolf, Denis Johnson, Steinbeck. I've read a lot of Willa Cather, a lot of García Márquez, a lot of Faulkner, a lot of James Baldwin. I tend to read writers who are highly stylistic and governed by a worldview that can't quite be articulated in familiar ways, writers who need to blend or transcend genres or traditions. But writers who, as *Driftwood* editors would agree is important, have a rhythm, a sense of what makes a sentence *theirs.*

Two writers whose novels I've been going through are Mohsin Hamid and Carlos Fuentes. Partly this is because I'm currently pursuing a PhD and am studying literary texts that deal with borderlands and transcultural experience, but also this is because their work tends to have everything I want in fiction: a strong narrative pull, intriguing and open-ended symbolism, a political bent, and crisp, vibrant prose.

But I also really wish I could write more like a Vonnegut, a George Saunders, or an Anne Lamott. That deadpan humor is so hard to achieve. And I appreciate it.

JM: Where can readers find more of your work? Have you been published before?

CF: I had a story come out last summer in *Red Earth Review,* called "Breath." A few years ago, I had a travel essay come out in *Fjords Review*, which is similar to "Work," meaning it arose out of my MFA manuscript; it deals with a different stretch of road, a search for Trementina Base, a site in New Mexico that is associated with Scientology.

JM: What are you working on now?

CF: A new story, in its early stages still, despite the time I've invested in it so far. I'm trying to map out a collection of connected stories. But I'm fighting the feeling that that is an artificial restriction at this stage in the process. Basically, I'm mostly busy trying to guard my schedule from competing obligations and, when I have time to work, I keep myself busy by tripping over myself.

JM: As we wrap up here, is there anything else you'd like to tell us about this work in particular? Any parting words?

CF: We talked a good bit about politics and autobiographical writing, which I love to talk about, but I'll just say quickly that writing is about the reader, not the writer. The reader illuminates the text, bringing unique, new meanings to it. So I'll thank the readers. And I'll thank you and your team at *Driftwood.* Y'all have been great to work with. And I appreciate all of the work—and I don't even know the half of it—that goes into editing and publishing.

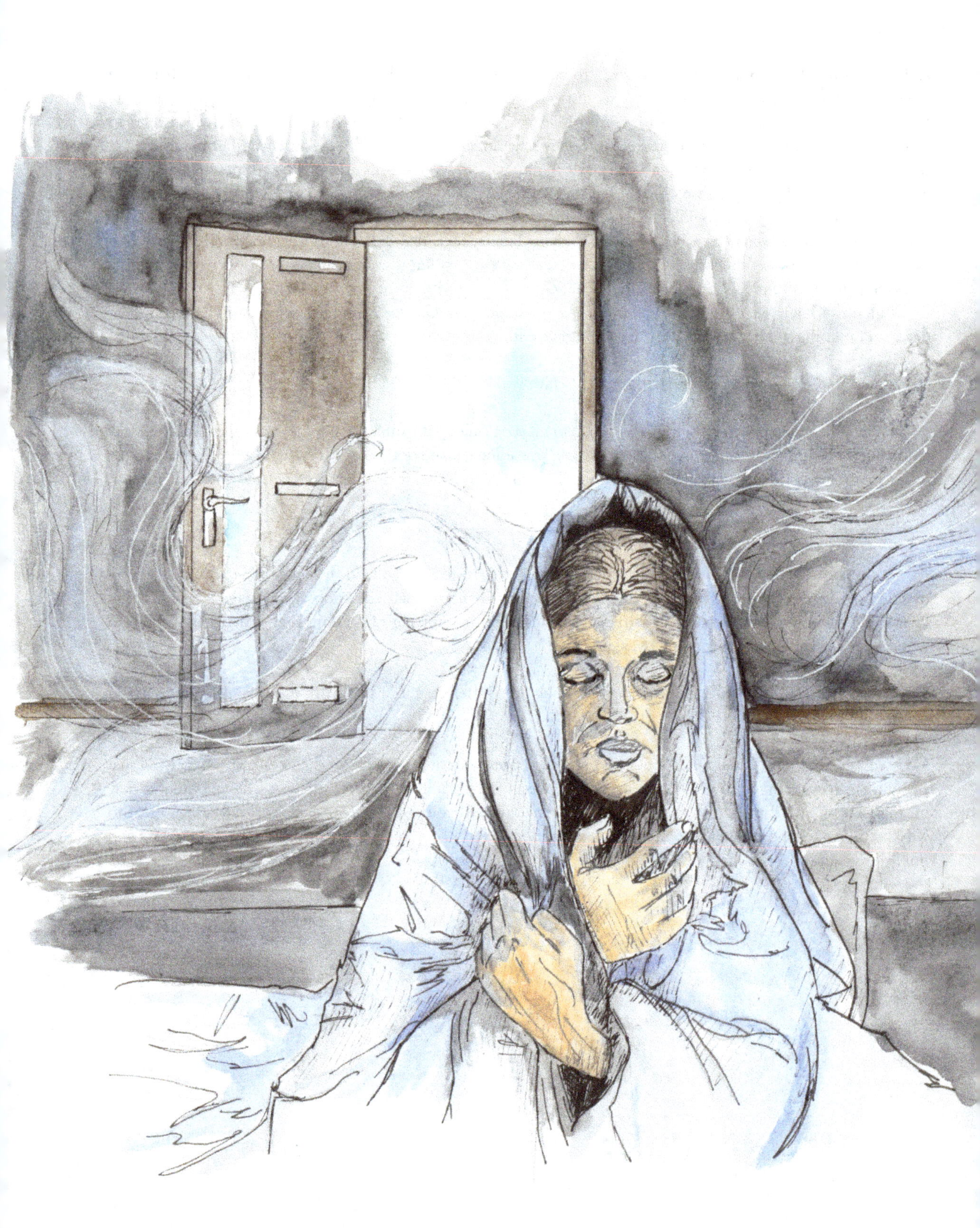

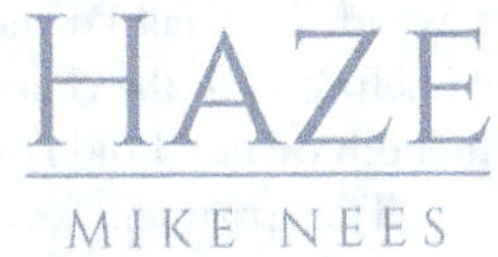

HAZE

MIKE NEES

"We need walls that'll keep that heat in," Gran kept saying.

"Entire building is vacuum-paneled," the landlord assured us. "Airtight." As we toured the rooms, Gran pushed her palms up against every surface she could reach, desperate to gauge the insulation. I wasn't sure if it made sense or not. I could only pray that she liked what she felt. Clean, well-lit—it'd been a long time since we were in an apartment this nice.

The landlord said he had more people coming to see it that afternoon. Halfway into the tour, in a kitchen full of big, new-looking appliances, a silence settled in. "We spent a year up in Duluth," Gran said. She told everyone about this. "This is years back, I'm talking. Found the greatest deal on a townhouse up there. Two floors, real nice. But the winter." Her scratchy voice always grated on me. "Cold just got in my bones and never left. Jesse could tell you—he has to put up with me now." She wrapped an icy hand around my forearm. "My body can't retain heat anymore. It's like a freak condition. Come winter, these walls don't insulate, I'll freeze to death."

I was four when we arrived in Duluth, thirteen now, and I'd yet to see her look anything but freezing. Even in the summers, she hid her bony frame under a mound of shawls. But the man who held the keys looked unsympathetic. I could feel our odds thinning the longer Gran spoke. "She's exaggerating," I said. Though not true to my knowledge, it came out in a steady, self-assured tone. I turned to Gran and added, calmly—as if I were joking: "Don't make us sound crazy."

I'd never talked to her like this before. I could feel her spine straighten, her jaws clenching. Though I'd been taller than her for years, I recall her looking down on me then. Glaring from up high.

Every winter she'd blast the heater, swaddle herself in blankets, and refuse to leave the house. On the coldest days, I'd come home from school to find an open oven broiling, Gran seated nearby. She'd gaze into it so intently that I never dared question her. If I sat down beside her, bore the heat with her, she might reminisce about the "good days" that I couldn't remember, before Duluth, when we lived in a warm house that bustled with friends. But her stories brought none of that back. Before long she'd find cracks in walls, or along the window frames, and insist that all the heat was escaping. Come summer, we'd move again.

But now, after glaring at me for so long that I regretted saying anything, she shrugged in surrender. "I guess it could be worse," she said. The landlord looked pleased to leave it at that. We were all business from there on, down to the final handshake. I couldn't believe it. Even as we drove home, a signed lease sliding around the backseat, Gran kept up a shrewd silence. It wasn't until the long red light at the SaveMore that she finally looked me over and said, "You're getting fresh."

I must've beamed. If I could just keep up that steady tone, I thought, I'd sway more developments now. Over our first pizza in the new apartment, I told Gran that I was tired of starting over. "It's not fair to me," I said, like someone who knew how to measure such a thing.

"This was the last move," she promised, staring at the blank kitchen walls. She'd promised this after the last "last move" too, and she conceded as much before I could point it out myself.

Her mind worked faster than most grownups'. Though wiry, and a bit hunched, she was only in her fifties—I'd seen kids my age with mothers as old. That fall I'd start High School, which meant my grades would count, and this too she acknowledged before I got the chance. "You're gonna get to focus here," she said. "We're gonna set down some roots, the both of us." I didn't trust her exactly, but I think I trusted the moment. Or I trusted myself to hold her to it. The apartment was "airtight," I reminded her.

On the first cold morning in our new apartment, Gran maxed the thermostat. Stepping out of my bedroom, I found her balled up on the couch, rocking back and forth. "No way any of this heat is getting out," I said, trying to project all the confidence I could. "It's just like the landlord said." Eyes on Judge Judy, Gran mumbled something non-committal.

The heater seemed to be doing its job, but I thought this about our previous heaters too, save for those we blew out. I would have to keep the mystique of our new walls alive, I was sure. I mentioned them as often as I could in the days that followed.

One night, hours after a shower, I returned to the bathroom to find the mirror still fogged, the air still bristling with moisture. It happened again the next day, and the day after that, until the mirror stopped clearing altogether. I started thinking back on how our skin used to crack in the winter—now my hands never seemed dry. Gran dismissed me at first, when I tried to point it all out. But soon it was undeniable: our apartment trapped the residue of every shower, run of the dishwasher, pot of boiled rice. It was airtight. "Like a sauna, right?"

"These walls are the real deal," she conceded.

A thick haze engulfed us. It grew stickier by the day, until Gran shed her cocoon of fabrics. I couldn't fathom what I was seeing. "Wet air conducts more heat," she said. One night, after I opened the kitchen window to let out a fly, she grieved, actually sobbed, for the haze that escaped along with it. I'd never made her cry before that, not that I can remember. She began to call out from the couch whenever I left the apartment: "Shut that door fast behind you." I had to slip in and out like a ghost.

The haze twisted our lampshades and floorboards, the corners of all the envelopes piled on the kitchen table. I rarely brought up the damage we were doing, and Gran winced in defense if I did. "I know," she'd say. "Just not now, alright?" I did my best to leave it alone.

There were things to be said for our new way of life. How the cloudy soup dulled our inhibitions. We wrote our names in the windows, stopped brushing the hair that stuck to our foreheads. We ate cookies by the sleeve, never minding the crumbs that fell out of view. But as it thickened, the haze warped more than just our fixtures. It refracted light and sound, casting mirages on itself. I walked past the bathroom one night to catch Gran roll a curling iron up and down her arms for warmth, humming something like a radio jingle. My mind adrift, I didn't even question it until the next day in Biology. Seated in the orderly lab, with all its un-fogged glass, I thought of what I'd seen—the punch-red streaks across her gaunt forearms—and I felt the blood drain from my face. It couldn't have been real, I thought. I remembered watching Mom twist her hair around a curling iron once, and how quickly she recoiled when it grazed the back of her neck. Though very old, the memory held strong. How bitterly she cursed.

During the first night of winter break, dizzy from the heat, I opened my bedroom window a crack, let the cold air slice through the haze for some twenty minutes. I was sure Gran would come banging on my door. But she didn't. I woke looser-limbed, feeling almost serene—unprepared for the sight of her brooding in the kitchen. She had the oven on broil, its scorching mouth agape. "You opened your window, didn't you?"

I didn't argue. It was too hot. Still, I must've made a face. "You think I'm full of shit," she said. I didn't know what I thought. "You're too young to remember who we were. Who I was. A bit rough around the edges, sure. But more dependable than anyone's husband. First person you'd leave your kids with." I grabbed a sweaty banana off the counter and collapsed in a chair beside her. Asked if I remembered the Salams, I shook my head. Gran gaped in disgust. "We babysat all their kids. You don't remember the birthdays they had at our house?"

As Gran invoked a house packed with friends of all ages, all of whom revolved around us—Me, her, and Mom—her tone relaxed. It was strange to me. Before now, her reminisces were terse, only ever seeming to push the past even further out of reach. But listening to her now, I saw the forgotten faces taking shape in the haze.

To help me understand how good we had it, she took me back to her "rough years," before she had Mom. She was drinking hard, she said. Smoking her voice into its current rasp. "But when your Mom came along, everything in my head just snapped into place. I was a saint from then on, anyone would tell you. Worked my ass off. No more bullshit, never fake with anyone. Who would've thought, right? But that's how it really happened."

As she recalled more names, some of Mom's friends came up. "The good ones," she made clear. Curious now, I tried to follow her, but I could only handle so many details—fragments of old friends would linger in the haze long after being mentioned. The old house, too, seemed to bleed into the present. I would rest my eyes on the flames snapping in our fireplace only to recall that we didn't have one, that Gran just kept mentioning the one we used to have. Like a rainbow in a sprinkler, it slid out of reach if I tried to approach it.

She spent the rest of winter break telling stories. She took big gulps of air between details, breathing life into each scene. Without the shawls, I could see her chest expand, the full body of machinery it required. But there was no stopping her.

When I went back to school, head spinning with Gran's stories, I struggled to follow the lectures on algebra and *The Crucible*. And when I got home after that first day back, Gran picked up a story right where she'd left off the night before: "…we all knew the poor kid was adopted, but we couldn't say a thing. God, he loved me."

I'd forgotten how this one started, and I had plenty of homework to do, but like most of her stories, it had its intrigue. I recalled something about a rigged school raffle. Tossing my backpack aside, I plopped down on the couch. I stared into the haze, watched it twist into wheels of tickets. A spinning raffle drum.

After dinner that night, I tried a conjuring of my own. I sat cross-legged in bed, took a deep breath, and let my thoughts sprawl like tentacles until one of them latched onto a distant memory: I'm sitting just like this, but beside Mom in some hibachi restaurant. We might've been celebrating something, I thought, though I didn't recall Gran there with us, or anyone else. In front of me, the haze twisted itself into an onion volcano. I recalled Mom's applause for the fire it spewed. But as she materialized beside me, the room seemed to contort. I heard the splintery writhing of timber. The walls were as bloated as everything else, I thought. As desperate to stretch.

The walk to school took me down a highway that reached straight into the horizon, traffic lights like notches on a ruler. Everything felt precise, calcified: the sharp angles of intersections, colossal fast food signs. Rudely, I'd glimpse the faces of people huddled under bus shelters. I'd feel the haze airing out of my head, though the process took longer every day.

Somewhere in January, unable to focus, I stopped talking in class. They made me see a counselor. Sitting down in his unadorned office, I found nothing to focus on but his face. More than half bald, he had an island of wispy hair, and a way of stressing certain words that pulled it closer into view. I did not seem "engaged," he told me. His questions sounded reasonable, as I recall, but the haze lived inside me now. My thoughts were vapor, wafting in all directions. After two sessions I agreed to go down a grade in Math, and he told me not to "disappear." He told me his door was "always open."

I learned to dedicate certain hours of the day to Gran, or else she would just blurt out memories as they came to her. Stories of people "we'd never see again," as she put it one day—though I saw them all the time now. The harder it got to spot Gran in the haze, the clearer I saw these strangers' faces. "Kaylee Henderson, total bitch. No other way to put it, sorry. Big money flaunter, how about that? And it's her daughter who turns your mom onto pills…" I heard these things daily now, without warning. "…I never gave her a reason to come after us. I knew how she was. But then she took her kids on a cruise and your mom robbed 'em all blind. Computers, jewelry. Everything."

She needed me to accompany her for each turn, to remind her of what led her down one tangent or another. Each hid its share of old comforts to plunder. The haze brimmed with these repossessions now: rowdy sleepovers, gossip over cake, a yellow lab with a fervent tail. I'd shimmy around it all, unfazed. Still curious at times. But by February we seemed to have covered all the "good days," and I feared what was left to thaw. I did my best to look away when Gran's eyes glistened.

Between commercials one night—well outside of the story time I established—Gran said that Mom got pregnant at twenty, the same age she had. I tried not to engage, but she kept talking about it, even after our show resumed. How she'd hoped I would force Mom to straighten out, the way Mom had for her. She rattled off the prices of all the rehabs she'd paid for, the legal fees when Mom went to court, the concessions she made to sell the house. The numbers meant nothing to me, but I felt the bite of each. Seeing Gran cringe through the corner of my eye, I turned to face her despite myself. But even then, clearly in pain, her eyes betrayed excitement. They seemed to widen every day.

My memory doesn't begin in earnest until those first days on our own, just me and Gran, up in Duluth. How we caught the hayride/costume contest on a whim, knowing no one else there, and Gran killed as Freddy. People came up to us all night to say she should've won. She met every kid's glance, said all the quotes with the bad words. And though her mask of melty flesh freaked me out, I recall admiring the power she commanded. How easily she tilted everyone in our favor. Even the monsters who climbed aboard the hayride to scare everyone else seemed to want nothing from us but friendship. They hung around for small talk before leaping back into the woods. The other riders congealed around me and Gran as the temperature dropped, and hugging her from the side, I felt her warmth through the fabric of her striped red sweater. But then she said something like, *See, we haven't forgotten how to have fun*, and it reminded me that Mom wouldn't be joining us.

I remember pulling a Cozy Coupe around the new development with my toes when a freezing wind blew through. Gran, raking our portion of the lawn, grimaced when it hit her, like someone stabbed on TV. It happened again as we walked home from the mechanic one afternoon, and she limped the rest of the way.

She still tried to lighten the mood, even as the cold crept under her skin. She recycled gossip from our previous life, though none of it filled the new home around us. We'd brought little with us, and never came close to filling the place. With all that empty space to insulate, it didn't seem so strange when she started hunting for cracks in the walls.

No longer wafting aimlessly, the haze churned with zeal by early March, always eager to finish Gran's thoughts for her. She trailed off one night while telling me about the preparation for one of Mom's sentencings, as if she'd thought better of it—but as the dress suit they picked out took shape before our eyes, sleeves winding like snakes through the air, Gran took a deep breath and pressed on. She recalled the measurements and price tag with longing, still knew which pant leg Mom snagged on the loose clip in the storm door on the morning of court, ripping it open at the thigh.

"I lost it," Gran said. "I started tearing out drawers, looking for a needle. And your Mom—" I saw Mom standing before us in her suit—"your mom just pulled me in for a hug. I was shaking in her arms, a total wreck. And she was so still. She just held me there. I had to push her back to get a look at her—" As Mom grew clearer in the haze, her face remained ablur, awaiting definition that Gran seemed to wrestle with. The surrounding air convulsed, impatient. I could hear the walls wrenching again, the whole living room twisting around the place Mom's face would be. "Let's watch TV," I said. But Gran wouldn't let it go. "I'm hungry," I said. "Let's order something."

"Just the deadest smile, Jesse."

Then I saw it: Mom's face emerged in front of us, her smile as flat as Gran's description. Dead. Gran shook her head at it. She bit her knuckle and turned away—finally, the haze relaxed. "I'm sorry," she said to me, choking up. I told her it was okay, eager to forget it.

But the walls kept groaning. They could only bend so far, I was sure. I heard them all that night. Over *Jerry Maguire,* as I brushed my teeth, turning over in bed: the walls refused to suffer in silence, and I was too exhausted to listen. I wished for a way to say, *I know. Just not now, alright?*

When I woke next, it was to the crack of a support beam, followed by the cacophony of my room collapsing in on itself. Something clubbed me in the head. Whatever piece of the building it was, I recall it feeling personal, like it was aiming for me.

I'm in a hospital, I thought. I'm sedated—but the air felt too hot. The mattress beneath me, too damp. When I opened my eyes, I found the usual blanket of haze bearing down on me, my beige walls intact. All that remained of my crushing was the sound of it. It kept ringing in my ears, even after I'd showered and dressed for school. It drowned out Gran as I shuffled out the door, didn't let up as I settled into homeroom. The sound of beams splitting like tree trunks all around me, too precise to have originated in my head—if it wasn't real yet, I was sure it would be soon.

When the final bell rung, and everyone scrambled to leave, I recalled the counselor who'd said his door was "always open." I could tell him I was living in a dangerous place, I thought. I imagined Gran, confronted by authorities, oversharing. She would self-deprecate, I was sure. While my story held steady, hers would twist and fray. I felt my self-assured voice returning to me, brewing in my lungs.

But despite his parting motto, I found the counselor's door closed. Among the notes taped to it: *Mr. Ferrone is in every first and third Wednesday.* I counted ten days until he'd be back.

Walking home, eyes on the half-shoveled sidewalks, I practiced my steady tone. We needed to open the windows, I would tell her. We'd pushed the walls too far. They wouldn't last another ten days.

I felt more than the usual pinch of dread for those uprooted slabs that led to our apartment. The prospect of confrontation exhausted me. But as I approached the front steps, my heart jolted: that morning, distracted, I'd left the door open. Snow now matted the foyer. The haze was gone. Slamming the door shut behind me, I ran into the living room to find the air as clear as the day we moved in. Blisters coated the ceiling, gray puddles filled the grooves in the floor, and atop the couch stood a heap of pillows and blankets that I flung behind me, digging my way to Gran. Colorless, wrapped in sheets, she looked almost larval. She responded to nothing I said. I shook her by the shoulders. "Couldn't make it to the door," she finally rasped. "Too cold."

My eyes watered with relief. I'd closed the door, I assured her. The haze would return—I could still taste it in the air. It would re-envelop us, I told her, and then she'd be okay. It wouldn't take too long.

"Open the oven," she begged. "Broil."

Still relieved, I didn't argue. I'll stay alert, I thought, walking to the kitchen, turning up the dial, opening the oven. It won't take long, I thought. When I returned to the living room, Gran was struggling to sit upright. I picked her up, carried her to the kitchen, and lowered her into a chair. She was lighter than my backpack. I felt like a giant. Her guardian. But after sitting down beside her, I glanced over to find her face still clenched in fear. "The organs aren't thawing," she said, hands clutching her sides. "I'm in a bad way, Jesse."

I made a point of staying calm. "I'll call an ambulance."

"There's no time." Her voice cracked on the word. "I'm freezing to death. What you gotta do is take that top rack out the oven, okay?" It took a moment to realize that I was being given instructions. "Jesse? Are you listening to me?"

I pictured her hugging the metal rack for warmth, couldn't make sense of it. But as I stared into our oven, the largest we ever had, I finally saw what she saw: with the rack removed, she could fit. She could move in, be its tenant. "Just for a few minutes," she said. "You gotta trust me, Jesse. Take the top rack out." I looked around for any signs of the haze returning. The air was too dry. "I'm freezing to death, Jesse. Don't you get it?"

Part of me got it, or thought I did. That bone-deep chill.

I pulled the top rack out with a dish rag. Gran told me where to find the big baking pan in the cabinet, and to set it down on the table. "Help me in," she said, once I had it out. For a moment I did nothing but stare down at her. "Don't fail me," she pled. "Help me in the pan, Jesse." She looked lost to me. I could see her among the faces under the bus shelters, speaking to no one. Looking at no one.

I didn't fail her. After helping her curl up in the pan, I lifted it off the table, eased her into the oven. On her side, glowing orange under the coils, she glared up at me. I watched without speaking, waiting for her to warm. "You're letting the heat out," she said. No, I thought. I felt my fingers going numb. "Remember this morning, Jesse? When I begged you to close the door?" My chest tightened at the thought of the open door, the snow in the foyer. She was right—I'd been stuck in my head all morning. And now I saw my trembling hand reach for the handle. "Don't open it until I knock," she said. "Not even a crack."

I closed the door. Waited for the knock. Somewhere in the back of my mind, I knew my composure had a short half-life. It would flicker out, because it had to. I would swing the door back open, yank the pan out with bare hands.

But time kept passing with no such panic. I heard Gran's final threat, over and over. *Not even a crack.*

I pictured the skin bubbling off her face. The ribbons of smoke twisting off her clothes.

My poise would crumble at any moment. My limbs would flood with panic. I kept telling myself this. I felt a thousand other selves swing the door open before I raised a finger. That I took so much longer than them—it said something dire about me. About this iteration of me I was birthing.

Because I knew what was happening. I could smell what I'd done—the charred and twisted body I would pull out of the oven, scorched to the bone in places. That I would scoop her out of the pan with shaking hands, preparing for her to crumble in my arms. And if she didn't, how I'd lay her down on the table's bed of letters, eyes fixed on her blackened chest, waiting for it to rise.

Overlapping Realities

A Conversation with Mike Nees

The following conversation was conducted by fiction editor Stephen Hundley.

Stephen Hundley: Hi, Mike. The fiction team and I were immediately drawn to the tangible atmosphere of "Haze." Can you speak to how you're using temperature?

Mike Nees: I think I started playing with temperature because of how quickly it can reorient us. If I stick my head out the window on a cold night, it feels like crossing into someone else's reality. It can be hard to believe in other people's lived experiences, especially as a kid, and so I'm interested in those visceral forces that jog the imagination, reminding us of the wide range of states that a body can be in.

SH: That visceral force pulls these scenes together.

There's a crisp sense of timing and compression to this story. What scenes were lost to the cutting room, and how do you go about making your scene selections in such a wild world?

MN: For a while I was trying to work in some of the main character's dreams. I imagined Jesse reading *The Crucible* at school and dreaming in colonial Salem. I also had Gran and Jesse try a church in their new neighborhood before the main events unfold. Writing those scenes probably helped me get a better sense of the characters, but in the end they felt too ornamental.

The biggest cut was to the end, where I originally had Jesse being interrogated by a detective over his actions in the story's climax. I was wrapped up in these interrogation analysis videos on YouTube at the time. It's funny to me now, how extraneous this sounds. I think I was still learning to trust the character. I wasn't ready to let his narration speak for itself yet. Once I had a stronger sense of him, it became clearer to me which plot points he would share, and which he would leave unspoken.

SH: What a great exercise. I've been coached to "ask" characters questions in a separate document, even to give them hypotheticals, but an out-and-out interrogation is something else! Put the squeeze on them.

So many of the images and scenes in "Haze" are fantastically gruesome. Gran rolling the curling iron over her arms. Beams bursting through the ceiling. Of course, the oven scene. I found myself wondering what was sincere and what was fever dream. Can you speak to managing reader disbelief?

MN: My own disbelief tends to hinge on my sense of an author's intent. If a story seems to bend reality in bad faith, it can be very jarring. But the same violation might work very well for me if that strangeness seems like an authentic expression of how reality feels. I think that's usually my intention when sharing my stranger visions with people.

I think existence is just really weird and convoluted when we're honest with ourselves, so it seems natural to try and validate a reader's own experience with that. It's also helpful that everyone seems to have this very intrinsic sense of when a story's spell wears off for them. An honest reader can often pinpoint the moment their disbelief wavers, and in my experience it's one of the first things they'll tell you. *I was with you for X and Y, but Z? I don't believe that.*

SH: Fair point and well said. We definitely have weirdness, but you render the extraordinary events with close humanity. I'm not sure which layer of the world this is happening in, but I do know I'm feeling it. And fruitful, artful-weirdness is hard to come by sometimes. Not weird for weird's sake, but demonstrating the character's paranoia or desire. It makes for an emotionally dense piece. Kind of humid.

You do a lovely job of blending scene and exposition in this story. How do you find this balance?

MN: Thank you. I find I personally have no problem skimming a story that drags its feet—I can remain engaged, if irritated, with long, drawn-out sequences—but the moment the author shoehorns some exposition in, I always seem to stop processing. So that's a red flag I look out for with my own writing. Have I just read an entire paragraph without absorbing it? Is there somewhere else where the reader would be better primed to process this information?

Reading exposition seems to require a different part of the brain, but I think that can make it a unique instrument to play with. It can hit some unexpected notes, if saved for the right moments. There are times when the mind wants to do more work than the story has assigned it, and a little new context can go a long way then. It's hard to plan for those moments, though, so I try to focus on momentum whenever in doubt.

SH: There's such a quiet momentum to this story. The characters arrive in a fairly closed environment. They don't do much traveling in the present tense. But there was a pressurized feel to the story. The conditions introduced a lot of potential energy, and I found myself waiting for the inciting tear. What would let the outside in. I love that when we get this tear—Jesse leaving the door open—it's driven by our main character.

It's satisfying to see a character make a mistake and come to a decision point before the story is over. Jesse puts Gran in a dangerous place. She positions herself for independence. We're wondering: What will she do? And readers are treated to three pages of resolving action—new material that must be character driven, must reflect on and advance the ten pages we've already read. You give yourself enough space to stick the landing without tying things up too much or, worse, rushing to a false epiphany. This story felt well measured.

In a story that thrives with very few characters, what makes the guidance counselor essential to this piece? Why is this our contact outside of the haze?

MN: After his little power play in the opening scene, Jesse doesn't get too many chances to assert himself. He's at that age where everything you do starts 'counting' (if it wasn't already), but at the same time, you're still kind of a pinball. You're at the whim of all these enormous forces. For Jesse, the guidance counselor is part of his story because he reinforces that increasingly strained pretense he's living under. He's supposed to have agency, but what does that really mean?

For me, the counselor also served as a way of maintaining the sense of 'fever dream,' you describe, as opposed to a restful dream. I wanted to assure the reader that this isn't the kind of story that just goes deeper and deeper into un-reality, until the stakes fizzle out. Jesse's choices do ultimately matter. Ideally, the dream-like aspects of Jesse's experience are balanced by a sense that the alarm clock could screech at any moment.

SH: That was my experience. I also enjoyed the grounding effect of the counselor brushes. A lot of what Jesse sees in the apartment is extraordinary, and even his past is semi-legendary, but, after we see him waiting outside the counselor's office, reaching out for that supposed agency and finding himself alone, our return to the house feels damned and doomed. It allows Jesse to carry a certain desperation that adds an edge to any illusions.

I want to praise the attention to detail in this piece. The movement of air. The dryness of a hand.

What, to your eye, makes a great detail in a short story? Where do you find your eye is drawn first or most naturally?

MN: Things in flux tend to draw my eye in real life. Churning clouds, fish tanks. I'm a sucker for lava lamps. We're always trying to make the body accept a state of stillness, but it knows we exist in this sloshy, dynamic world, and how small fluctuations can announce bigger, dramatic changes. I think that's another part of what kept me coming back to the literal climate of "Haze."

I think great details in short stories don't just excite the senses, but also ask compelling questions that may or may not get answered. As in real life, it shouldn't be too easy to guess which of our little observations will prove to be crucial in the end. But that shouldn't stop us from guessing.

A friend is writing a story in which a woman drops a cookie on the floor but returns it to the cookie plate unbeknownst to her housemates. I don't think the cookie factors into the story after that, but the brief description of it on the floor infused the object with all this potential energy. Who's going to eat the floor-cookie? I think a lot of the author's work goes into juggling these secondary questions, or else we risk a sense of flatness.

SH: Agreed. I feel that juggling sensation as a writer and a reader when I see a sparking detail. My brain is holding it, waiting to see how it informs character and conflict. It's a joy when details like the cookie or the counselor form an environment of reactions to the character. They give the feeling of a world responding.

The story leaves us with Gran still in the oven and the protagonist in something of a daze. What does this ending evoke for you? Where does it bring you, emotionally or otherwise, and why is it important you let the curtain fall where you do?

MN: I resisted it for a while. Loss is so central to the story, it felt right to linger on the aftermath of this scene. It also seemed cruel to freeze Jesse in it. But something about the conceit of their overlapping realities, his and Gran's, seemed to prohibit the story from outliving her. I suppose their entanglement is a part of the story's spell, going back to what we were saying about disbelief, and so it probably makes sense that the spell would wear off once one of them is removed.

There are so many traumas that seep through generations, and we too often ignore the plain fact of this. It's easier to believe that every kid gets a blank slate on which to write their story. I wanted to stress the contradiction of this line of thought, and I hope this ending does that. Jesse is still clinging to the hope that he might not be alone in the world. That seems to say more about his plight than any further narrative would provide.

SH: Overlapping realities. That's a beautiful way of putting it. You made the apartment spell from Gran, and in a story with traveler-type characters, you made the site of the story feel like a terminus and a breaking point. There was the Duluth time before, but this is the most important time for Jesse.

One of the benefits of having a story-telling character like Gran is the robust backstory that is pushing these characters around. It's compelling. Did you ever experiment with different POVs or entry points with this story? You do well to place us at a moment of choice for Jesse. Still, I found myself really curious about Mom's decline and Gran's golden years. Ever considered revisiting these characters or expanding this, or have you worked with these characters/places before?

MN: In my first draft, I think the opening was just a description of all the stuff in their apartment getting warped by the haze. I found that rewinding to their first glimpse of the place, the viewing, made the story feel more inviting.

With each piece I start, I usually feel the need to make everything from scratch. I have respect for authors who can revisit their characters in engaging ways, but the stories I'm writing lately seem to benefit from self-containment. I do strive to make my characters seaworthy, so to speak—I don't want their potential to seem confined to whichever story I happen to dock them in—but I've never felt like the kind of writer who would shine the biggest, brightest spotlight on my subjects, either. To write like a biographer. I'm exposed to such a deluge of intimate stories from so many walks of life in my day job as a case manager, I think it's made me a little less eager to plot the broader arcs of people's lives, or to try and master the story of any one life. I'm sure I'll try to do more of that eventually, for better or worse, but I think my interests are more impressionistic right now.

SH: Could you speak to your drafting and editing process? How many drafts did this story see before it was published?

MN: I have to make an effort not to get too deep in the weeds with early drafts. I have a habit of revising paragraphs into oblivion, which can be a huge waste of energy, since there's always the chance that I'll take a step back, re-envision a story, and cut what I've revised anyway. So overall I think my process involves a lot up-close tinkering, punctuated by periodic steps back to rethink the bigger picture.

SH: What authors or pieces do you consider your work, and "Haze" specifically, to be in conversation with?

MN: The big-time magical realists like Marquez and Rushdie were intoxicating to me in my late teens and early twenties, but the short stories of Aimee Bender were what really inspired me to explore my own stranger impulses. I'd say "Haze" is a distant relative of her story, "Dearth." A story called "Somewhere in Bombay, a Fog Descends," by Asha Thanki was also on my mind. Finally, I was thinking about stories from my own mom and grandmother, who themselves grew up in the kind of tight-knit community that demands reminiscence.

SH: What are you reading?

MN: I recently finished Colson Whitehead's outstanding *Nickel Boys*, and I'm currently enjoying stories from Angela Carter's collection, *The Bloody Chamber*, and Randall Kenan's *If I had Two Wings*. I was also recently persuaded by a friend's enthusiasm for *Jane Eyre* to give that classic a shot. As someone who generally sticks to contemporary fiction and sort of expected a slog, I have to admit that it was actually pretty bonkers. Quite the thrill ride.

SH: What are you working on now, and where else can we find your work?

MN: I'm hoping to assemble a book-length collection of surreal and speculative shorts that explore our perceptions of reality and the social structures we use to enforce them. Links to recently published stories about time dilation, solar flare, mind grafting, and bees can be found on my website (storyslamac.com/nees).

SH: As we wrap up here, is there anything else you'd like to tell us about this work in particular? Any parting words?

MN: I'm excited to see "Haze" in *Driftwood.* When writing a story like this, it's incredibly helpful to know that there are publishers out there willing to take a walk on the wild side, and to curate their findings with the kind of love and attention that one sees in these pages.

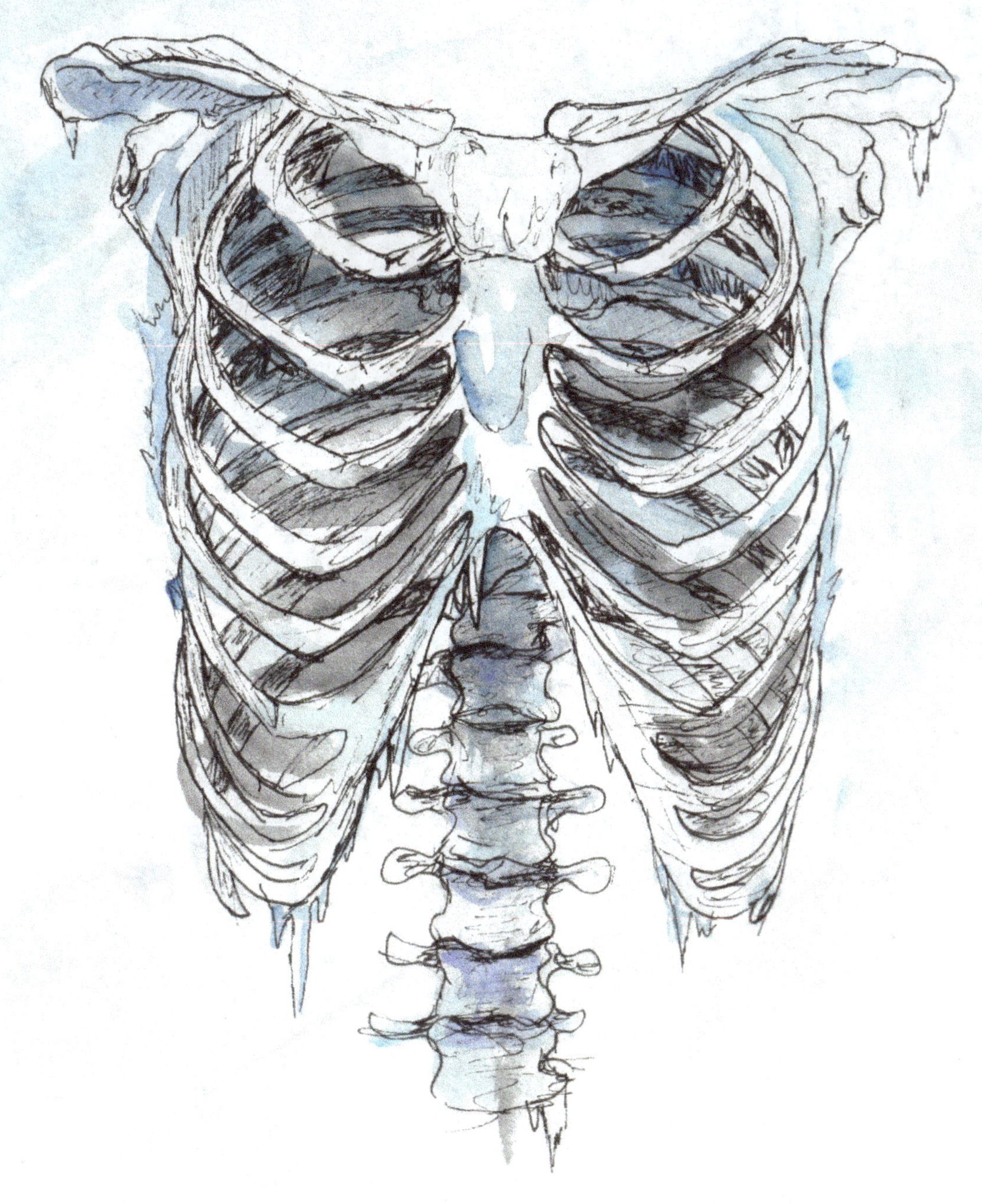

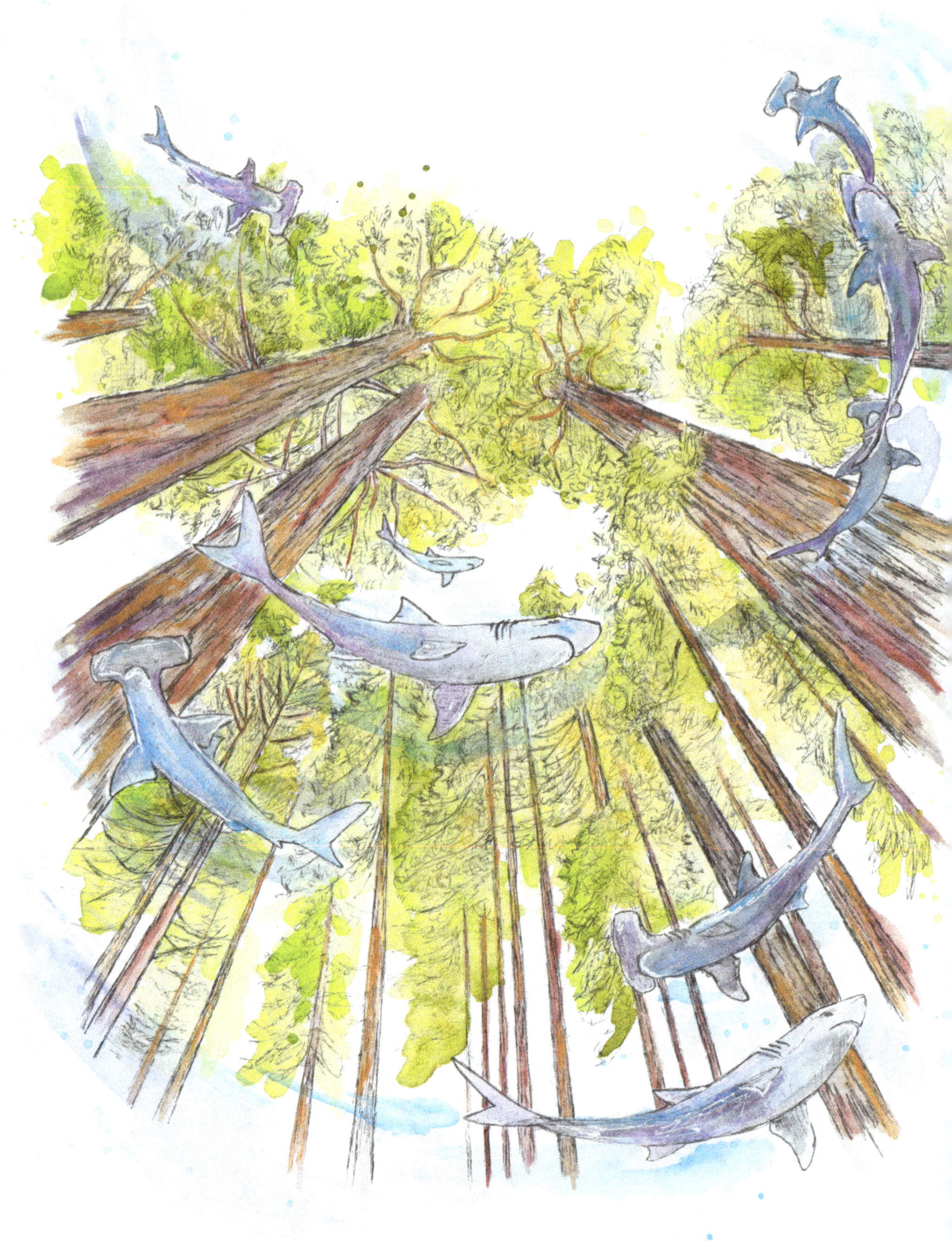

The Year of the Wood Sheep

LEIGH LUCAS

I once lived measured and cut, rigid among fish. I read the same books over and over; I ate oats in bed. Then came the Year of the Splash. Then came the Year of the Fog. And the Storm. Then the Year

of Forgetting.
This is the year I recover from the blast.

A spinning globe leads my way as I track Aurora Borealis, as I learn to speak in tongues and lick the paws of those who've left me.
For me

the redwoods quake, the shark swims and the baby says *uh oh.* Gracing spaces, I drop a shadow as big as anyone
casts, then bigger. I will not
ask myself how to read in the dark. Or how your mouth, silent as a cat's, spoke to me how the only way I've ever heard it: *there you are there there you are.*

INTERVIEW
WITH LEIGH LUCAS

Before we get into specifics, I wanted to open the interview by asking what the onus for this poem was? To be frank, I was floored by the mix of mystery and concrete details in your piece, and I would love to know what the writing looked like in its infancy.

Thanks for the kind words about my work! I'm honored that you and the editorial team chose my poem, so thank you.

I set out to write my own kind of blessing, creed, or incantation, one not rooted in the religion or traditions I grew up with, but invented from my own lived experiences and my mind's collection of images. Something a little like "may the road rise to meet you..." but authentic for me.

In its infancy, this piece was way longer; I cut and cut and cut. Now some moments in the poem happen in just a flash.

Time, specifically the passage of certain years, is a crucial component of the poem. How did you come at each year mentioned in this poem, and can you expound upon their significance for the poem's speaker?

The second half of my 20s was a wild ride. At twenty-six, I lost a loved one, and in the years that followed I had to emerge from my grief and get along with the new person I had become. That initial loss transformed into confusion (Fog), anger (Storm), and what felt like a second death—the dulling of details of how he moved, looked, laughed. Additionally, once a loved one's absence has become such an enormous presence in your life, the fading of grief is also painful.

The steady assuredness and calm nature of my now fiance has done wonderful things for helping me live in the moment by being someone who does this naturally. I also did the work to get there myself. Something I try to remember is that the Sliding Doors concept is just that—a concept!—there is no second version of your life: having better luck or making better choices. It is important to stay attentive to your own story, which belongs entirely to you. Each of us has the privilege of enjoying every moment.

The visual language is one of my favorite elements in this poem, moving effortlessly from prose blocks to purposeful line/stanza breaks. How did you approach form and visuals when writing this piece?

I used to make all of my line breaks by gut until I read *The Art of the Poetic Line* by James Longenbach. Now I think a lot about where I want my reader to speed up, slow down, or breathe. I wanted this piece to look more like a prayer than a poem. I wanted the reader to be able to really hear the baby say "uh oh." Babies are always little promises of hope. While I'm not sure I accomplished that, I did think about it a lot.

Having read through the poem multiple times, I keep leaving with the awestruck feeling that I've just read a fable; maybe more specifically, there are moments of universal community and honesty throughout the piece. What kinds of honesty did you want to communicate here?

No matter what happened in your past, or the uncertainties of your future, the present moment is always survivable, and it's almost always beautiful too.

What poets, writers, or artists were the biggest in-

fluence on this poem specifically?

My artist friends. When I was a little kid, I dreamed about being part of a riotous group of artists who rode around together in a van. For whatever reason, my role in this fantasy was that of the sax player (I have never picked up a saxophone). I did end up making some artist friends, but the rest played out very differently, which is for the best.

Amy Lin is a fiction writer who has taught me everything I know about delicious detail. My painter friend Jamie Corley is my inspiration for combining the gothic and the exuberant. My friend Hieu Minh Nguyen is a poet who taught me that vulnerable writing is the best writing.

Is this poem categorical of your work? Why or why not?

I have always admired artists who defy categorization. I want to keep discovering what a "Leigh poem" looks like, make a habit of creating work that surprises me.

If you had to narrow it down, what three books have had the most impact on your writing?

Autobiography of Red & *Nox,* both by Anne Carson. *The Chronology of Water* by Lidia Yuknavitch. These books taught me to always strive to be a wild writer.

Based on your personal experience, what advice would you give to other writers?

Write from your weirdest self. Worry about what people might think later (or never. If you can pull that off, tell me how).

What I Know of Strangulation

Heidi Seaborn

I know the word wedges
like poorly chewed meat
in the throttle the gullet the throat

I know how fruit is bruised
and short grass trampled

I know when a choke berry blooms
and white blossoms
become blood red berries

how my rapist must have leaned away
to admire such beauty
made with his own hands

my neck is a pedestal
and on my back a pair of wings

I know when the noose of his fingers
loosened

stars caught in my throat
I inhaled

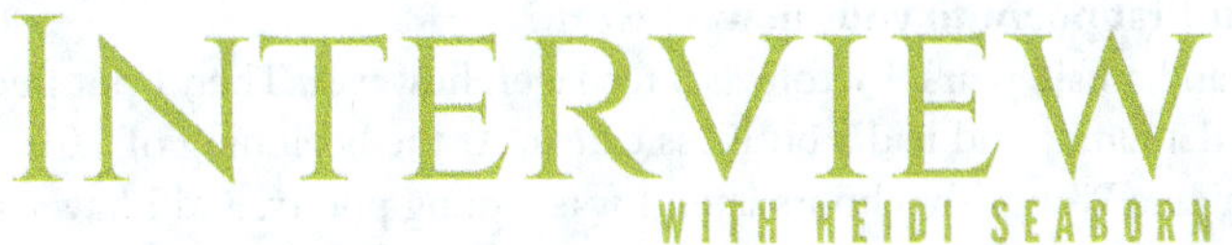

INTERVIEW
WITH HEIDI SEABORN

What inspired the poem?

Last summer when George Floyd was murdered by strangulation, I, like most of the world, was horrified and angry. But that event also brought up visceral, physical memories of my own strangulation that occurred when I was kidnapped, raped, and strangled when I was twelve.

What was the hardest part about writing it?

The hardest part was before I wrote the poem. Letting those memories stir alive in my mind, having them sit together with George Floyd's heartbreaking end. Once I turned to the page, my focus was on the poem. So often, the very act of writing is the most healing gesture.

What came easiest when writing this poem?

The title and the opening. Because the poem was a direct response to a current situation, I started with that, that I know what it feels like to be strangled. But I also don't know, could never know, what it's like to be a black man strangled to death by a police officer. By defining the range of knowledge of the speaker and emphasizing it with the anaphora, I cordoned off the knowing from the unknowing.

Was there anything in your original conception that did not make it in?

Yes, the initial spill of words encompassed what I didn't know. I tried to negate my knowing. But that was a failure.

How much revision went into this poem?

I brought the raw form of it, roughly lineated to a weekly workshop I have on Sunday mornings. And I received good input, in particular from a poet that I often pass work back and forth with. She saw the tighter, less sprawling version of this poem and guided me to it. Then it was easy, as I love revision and am quite good at taking a scalpel to my work. So, one pass was really all it took.

Is this poem categorical of your work? Why or why not?

Yes, in that I rely on and often return to imagery from the body and nature for inspiration. No, in that for me each poem is unique. Even in a series, I see them as separate creatures that will grow up to be distinct.

What is your favorite line from the poem or the line you are most proud of?

"my neck is a pedestal"

When I wrote this line, I was thinking of the shape of the neck. But it takes on another layer of meaning following the previous stanza. The rapist becomes an artist. The head enters without ever being identified—is it there at all? Then that line sets up the next line, which might evoke the "Winged Victory" for the reader—a sculpted woman, headless—just a body to be defiled.

Is there anything unique about your personal writing process?

I'm fast. Generally, I write quickly, put the poem aside for a day or two, then return and revise and revise until I think it's done. I might share it in a workshop or with a friend to see what's not working. But generally, the time from writing to submitting is a couple weeks at most.

How long have you been writing poetry? What

has changed from your first poem to your newest work?

Since 2016, so five and a half years. I wrote as a teenager, however. Then I put poetry aside for forty years. During that time, I raised a family and had a business career. At the beginning of 2016, I decided to take a class at the Hugo House with Jane Wong. Two hours later, I was writing poetry, and I haven't stopped.

Based on your personal experience, what advice would you give to other writers?

As Executive Editor at *Adroit*, and having just finished an MFA (NYU), I'm surrounded by young writers who feel immense pressure for success. To that, I say, there's not a rush. You can go off and do other things, live a different life. The poetry is always there, in your gut. When you are ready, it will come. And to older people like myself I say, what are you waiting for?

What is the best piece of writing advice you've been given?

As I came back to writing after the forty-year hiatus, I was able to study for a couple years with David Wagoner. His advice—there are three stages to writing: the madman, the editor, and the critic. Too often we let our critic mind in too early in our process. Even as someone who writes quickly, I try to honor those stages, to bring the right mind to the work at the right time.

My thesis advisor, Catherine Barnett, forced me to write every day. It's not something I enjoy or that I can say I do—but when I do, it is highly productive.

Where can readers find more of your work?

I have a new chapbook out, *Bite Marks*, that won the Comstock Review Award. And my second full-length collection *An Insomniac's Slumber Party with Marilyn Monroe*, which won the PANK Poetry Prize, is able to be preordered for a June 1, 2021 publication date. And of course, my website (heidiseabornpoet.com).

What drew you to *Driftwood Press*?

When I first started writing, I came across *Driftwood Press*. First of all, everything *Driftwood* produces is visually stunning and I loved the work. I also have read a couple of your books. I submitted a couple times, and finally, I sent along a poem that clicked!

The Wedding

Rachel Marie Patterson

We held each other under an oak tree
disfigured by lightning. The dog chafed
in her stiff, purple dress as white smoke
circled the earth. Meanwhile the caterer
found your brother on the couch and pressed
her hand to his face to see if he was breathing.
We laughed in a downpour of lavender seeds
as frogs went extinct. The great bowl of grief
is decorated with mirrors and candied violets.
Under a white tarp on a brick patio, we danced,
thinking of nobody but ourselves.

Beneath the Exam Table

Samantha Deflitch

Slowly up, I lifted my hand.
Under my hand was a city and
under the city was Marge's house.
Under this house was rust.
Under the rust was my hand
and the crack in my hand was
long and it was very firm
and it was big as a dynasty.
It was the color of the Ohio.

Remember what Marge
made? It was like a casserole
with pork, corn, and potatoes.
Does anyone have the recipe?
It was very good and she
served it with canned pears.
It was very good and it tasted
like backally bridge in the church
basement under an old crucifix.

I'm serious: if anyone has Marge's
recipe for pork, corn, and potatoes
send it to me. I'm not hard to find.
I'm also under the old crucifix
asking for a miracle. A miracle
is like when Mark, who's working
in the St. Agnes kitchen during
the Lenten fish fry, gives you extra
halushki at the end of the night.

Funny, to have this whole city
under my hand: St. Agnes in Irwin
and Marge's house in Mt. Pleasant,
the Strip District and Hot Metal
Street Bridge. My mother's kitchen
and its window, looking over the
snow-tracked backyard where my
father stares at the cracked sky. It's
a very small palm. I cross myself.

Gently, I set my hand back down
so as not to disturb Uncle Don
who has just sat down to play
cards at the folding table in old
Marge's house. There is a nut roll
long time cooling on the counter.
Uncle Don shuffles. This would
be his last winter, and he was
again going to rig the score.

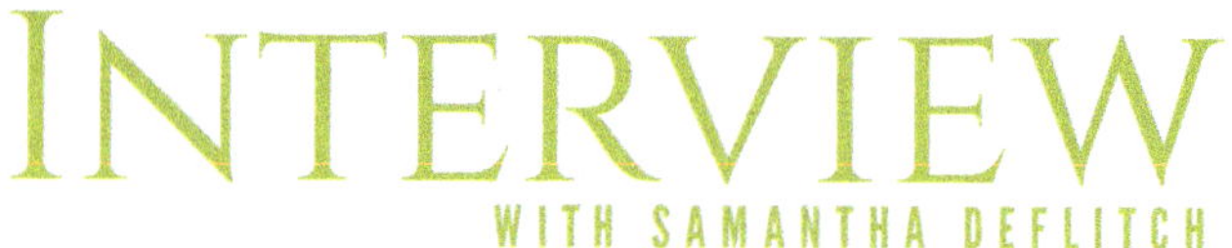

INTERVIEW WITH SAMANTHA DEFLITCH

What inspired the poem?

A few months before writing the poem, my mother told me a story about a family member (the Uncle Don of the last stanza) who apparently had his own method of scoring games of back alley bridge (read: he probably cheated a little bit). I had tried several ways of coaxing that story into a poem before this poem emerged; the last stanza felt very much like a natural place for the story to rest.

What was the hardest part about writing it?

The tenses, especially in the last stanza. It was actually a really tricky piece of work; it starts in past tense but shifts to present, then present continuous, then a conditional. (I'm pretty sure I got all that right; don't quote me, though!) There needed to be a sense that this action was ongoing; that the card playing, nut roll cooling, and rigging the score were always happening in this place. I think getting the tenses just right helped me with that.

What came easiest when writing this poem?

The movement. Starting the poem with a gesture did a lot of work for me; from there, I was able to build three stanzas before returning to the gesturing hand (a sign of the cross) and the lowering of the hand on the final stanza. The title also came very easily (which is not usually the case for me!). I had just written a poem called "On the Exam Table" and this poem, while very different content-wise, felt like a natural extension of that poem. Once the hand lifted, I thought, "lifted from what?" The answer, it turned out, was from the exam table.

Is this poem categorical of your work? Why or why not?

Yes, especially with regard to content. I would certainly say (at least, right now) I am a poet of place, and that place is Western Pennsylvania. I'm very interested in a poem that says, "I am this place"—not a representation of place, and here I'm working with movement to try and accomplish that. Many of my obsessions have also made it into the poem, including hand movements—especially practiced and sacred hand movements, everything from the sign of the cross to shuffling cards.

What is your favorite line from the poem or the line you are most proud of?

"My mother's kitchen / and it's window, looking over the / snow-tracked backyard where my / father stares at the cracked sky."

This is actually in conversation with the poem "Crossing the Hot Metal Street Bridge" from my book *Confluence*; in that poem, my mother is frying pierogies and she gazes out the kitchen window, where my father is carrying an old dog in his arms. In "Beneath the Exam Table," though, there is no dog; she has passed on. This is the gentle passage of time that is a central theme in the poem.

If you had to narrow it down, what three books have had the most impact on your writing?

Ada Limon's *The Carrying,* Charles Simic's *The Lunatic,* and *A God in the House: Poets Talk About Faith* edited by Ilya Kaminsky and Katherine Towler.

'THE TONGUE ALSO IS A FIRE, A WORLD'

BLAIR BENJAMIN

No human being can tame the tongue.
—Book of James, Chapter 3

Tongue-tangled like a Gordian knot,
dried and wrung of speech.
Picture it this, a slow-stepper, a little
arched, plated water bear on its eight
clawed legs, dessicated—
no, not an extremophile: a survivor.
Maybe it contains a world
of iniquity, or gentleness, or mystery.
Might its parched folds
hold a miniature litany of creation?
How would you know
unless you trained your microscope,
held your dropper at the proper angle,
squeezed a bit and let the stilled
yet not-dead tongue creep back to life?

Streak of Bitterness
A Wave

SUSAN BRUCE

I decide all matters regarding me, dark and in a hurry every morning of history.

The complication is my streak of bitterness widening in the currents.

I say what I think. I call myself the least conscientious, the most unwoven wave.

Flies / compulsion / desire / forgetting. Death is just another coffin.

Have I ever loved nighttime? *No.* The unseeable feels pointless and fatal.

Have I ever stayed more than one night in any one place? *No.*

Can I exist alone and lined up for one night only? *No.*

You cannot even lift me up or move me to the side.

It is unbearable to see my reckless tenderness.

All I want to do is take care of life. Instead, I stare away all hours.

My nature stops me from saying *Please swim with me.*

INTERVIEW

WITH SUSAN BRUCE

What inspired the poem?

I'm writing all my poems during COVID "as a wave" and in first person. Why am I doing that? Because swimming makes me happy and I need that now, because water is freeing and 2020 was not.

Was there anything in your original conception that did not make it in?

I'd say that because I'm anthropomorphizing I delete a lot of lines, words that border on hokey or sweet.

I revise a lot. It takes time for me to discover the surprises and even what I'm trying to say.

Is this poem categorical of your work? Why or why not?

I verge on writing about literal life—what I'm going through. As I layer in images, the images sort of liberate and loosen up the specifics in my writing and the meaning begins to broaden.

What is your favorite line from the poem or the line you are most proud of?

My nature stops me from saying, "*Please swim with me.*"

This line references the isolation of COVID. I see the waves in parallel formation, socially distanced and unable to actually come in close contact.

I recognize my need to be in connection, connecting.

Is there anything unique about your personal writing process?

I pull words from magazines, newspapers, fiction—words that I would never use or even think of using.

How long do you usually spend working on a single poem?

One week. But if I'm not still not satisfied, it means I'm obsessing and I need to put it down for awhile and come back to it later.

How long have you been writing poetry? What has changed from your first poem to your newest work?

I've been "emerging" as a poet since 1999. I don't have an MFA in writing.

I have an MFA in Acting and ¾ of a masters in teaching. My first poem was about water filling up my living room. My subject matter has continued, but now I search for images and metaphors instead of using only my feelings.

Who are some of your favorite poets?

John Ashbery, Sharon Olds, Marie Howe, Alan Dugan, Mark Strand, Alice Notley, Bob Dylan, Joni Mitchell, and Adrienne Rich.

How would you personally define poetry?

A moment explored or invented. A question realized and exposed.

Based on your personal experience, what advice would you give to other writers?

Read and underline in books or magazines what jumps out at you. Listen to how people talk and what they say. Steal language if it captivates you. Take yourself and your thoughts seriously. Listen to your thoughts with curiosity. Write it all down. Then write a poem.

What is the best piece of writing advice you've been given?

"It takes twenty years to do anything well." -Sandy Meisner

Grandma Dolores: The Prophet

TAYLOR CRAYTON

Under the shade of hawk-infested trees I walk
down my block to Freezy Street, while my brother moves
along with my shadow, thumping his feet
on every brittle leaf left on the burnt pavement.

I used to do the same on the cracked concrete
running in front Maw Maw's house when I was a child.
She used to sit on her porch throwing clumps of bread
at the fighting chickens in her yard, stopping every so often
to dab droplets of sweat from her brow.

In the summer, someone is gonna die.
I remember the words cleanly spoken
from the lips of Grandma Dolores as she rested
in her queen bed, her body slowly letting go of itself.
Momma always said that the women in our family were prophets.

I pause on the sidewalk. Somebody is screaming.
Behind me, my brother kneels in a flower patch picking
all the blue petals he can find while cop cars flood our block,
their sirens barreling through my body like gunshots.

Grabbing my brother by his dirt-stained Thomas the Train shirt,
I run with the cop cars heading to our house. Humidity pulls
my skin tight while the wind whips my ears. I tuck
this image: a black girl holding a black boy with flowers.

On the other side of the street, a group of crows
congregate in a circle near the neighborhood church.
Their black beaks pointed toward the sky, as if
they too needed to ask God a question.

Today marks the first day of summer in New Orleans.

Self Portrait as Miss High and Mighty

ANNA LEIGH KNOWLES

Her neck is a patched birthday quilt from Laverne
& her hair is a fistful of swizzle sticks from every bar Bud ever went
& her wrists are cold belt buckles
& her moles are flickering leaves
& her lazy eye is a lavender-tinted mirror
& her knuckles are the spires of St. Ignace the day Bud and Laverne married
& her laughter is the pang of the gut bucket
& her eye-lids are bacon grease splashed across Laverne's apron
& her kneecaps are mounds of cool whip
& her eyes are wisteria wheeling inside Bernheim forest
& her teeth are a deck of cards
& her fingernails are Uncle John's silver tokens from Caesar's Palace
& her cheeks are a sweep of passing headlights down Magnolia
& her elbows are the busted gravestones in Highland Cemetery
& her forearms are the slick estuaries of the Green River
& her eyebrows are tufts of jimsonweed wilting along L&N cars
& her eyelashes are the steel beams of the Big 4
& her touch is pine sap settled over cold rain
& her cough is Uncle Bill's busted muffler
& her earlobes are limestone cuts dissolved into the riverbank
& her callouses are brown roses
& her tongue is Bud's old bowling ball
& her shame is a yellowing letter
& her shadow is a blue jean jacket
& her lungs are radios announcing tornadoes
& her frown is the engine grill of Grandma Marilyn's parked 1957 Chevy
& her skin is cracked wallpaper depicting large clouds
& her worry is the combustion of stars
& her legs are cots pushed together for sleeping
& her prayers are thin denim shirts
& her sigh is a heavy old bicycle
& her thumbs are loose doorjambs
& her throat is one of Bud's shirtsleeves pulled up tight
And when they told her, you're too big for this place

what could she have done—pretend not to hear
the loss assemble like an orchestra in the pit?

Who thinks of this girl anymore?
The one grown heavy with incident and time?

The one consumed by seasons of mud and sweltering mirage?
Who lifts the swoon of her insistent dreams?

Who thinks of the haunted woman she's become?
Her want, a promise to die early

if it means light above the tar shingles,
a gallery of wonderful omens at the heart's hot core.

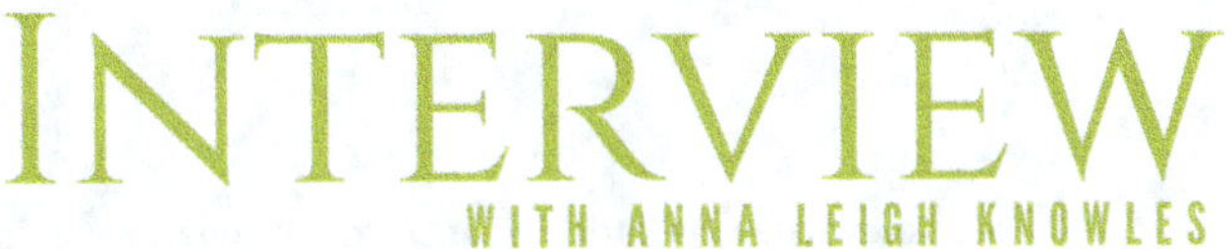

What inspired the poem?

The poem was inspired during an online workshop with Ohio poet laureate Kari Gunter-Seymour, who I was lucky to work with during last year's Appalachian Writers Workshop. I was thinking about how to insert more of myself into my current manuscript—how to manifest my need to be present in spaces I find myself more and more removed from. Re-imagining myself through objects and images I already feel attached to made sense to me.

What was the hardest part about writing it?

This was the first self-portrait poem I have ever written, so the hardest part was letting myself do something new aside from lyric-narrative poems.

Was there anything in your original conception that did not make it in?

At times I wanted the metaphor to take more charge and space, and other times I wanted the couplets to never end. So the poem became what it was because I needed to stop myself at some point and control the images by building the couplets almost like a landing pad.

How much revision went into this poem?

I worked on this one for about six or seven months. Most of the revision was tweaking small things, parts of images, ideas, and sentiments within the couplets. Cutting back.

Is this poem categorical of your work? Why or why not?

I wouldn't say so. I think this is the most different, strangest poem I have ever written.

What is your favorite line from the poem or the line you are most proud of?

"Her want—a promise to die early." I've been thinking about that line for a long time. The truth behind it scared me—and still does.

How long do you usually spend working on a single poem?

That depends on the poem. Some poems I have been working on for over seven years. Some poems I write in weeks. The poems I think about for too long are usually the ones that take the longest time to write.

How long have you been writing poetry? What has changed from your first poem to your newest work?

I wrote terrible poetry for about eight years before I learned how to get a story down. I would like to think that I am more clear now, that the poems have more groundedness but also adhere to my natural inclination toward the lyric.

Who are some of your favorite poets?

Lynda Hull, Anne Michaels, Anne Caston, Nickole Brown, and so many others.

If you had to narrow it down, what three books have had the most impact on your writing?

Nickole Brown's *Fanny Says,* Anne Caston's *Flying Out With The Wounded,* & Lynda Hull's *Ghost Money.*

REYKJAVIK SERMON

TESSA LIVINGSTONE

Please acknowledge my knocking on. Acknowledge an opening so small, at first you hardly noticed. Notice now, the smallness of Reykjavik. The smallness of harbors. Of fish, slathered in butter. How you can get lost and easily be found.

Consider the smallness of this room. The cold metal table. The dog, on the floor, in her bed. The vet on his knees. Consider how things are decided. Consider this the room where things are decided. Consider the IV in her leg. The shape of the IV in her leg. The shape of her skull. One side of the skull is never exactly like the other. Consider your arm. How a limb is joined to the body. Glue, made from the bones and skins of cows. Consider the container ship, carrying cattle. Pens on the open decks. Their brown eyes, six times too large. Their bodies, to be opened at the throats. Their faces. The flies on their faces.

Consider what the captain fed you. The scraping of lips, of nose, of bone. And how long it took you to look at horses. After you saw Dundee's intestines, tumbling, ribboning red. All them lovely horses. Consider how you hardly looked at them at all. Get into the habit of looking at cows. Your dog. Consider her dying. Consider always someone touching her. Infinity as scientific fact. Consider the Egyptians, who carved their sacred cats in wood. Remember many things carved from wood. Furniture, plain and undecorated. Heavy doors that won't stay shut.

Consider the first sign of rapping, or splitting. You can arrange that it's cut away. Consider cutting away doors that won't stay shut. Their corners, removed by saws. Consider a sharp chisel when removing small pieces of wood. *I must not take too much. I cannot put it back.* Consider taking too much, and putting it back. Consider people with headaches or toothaches. The cows and your dog. The smallness of Reykjavik. The vet who got down on his knees.

INTERVIEW

WITH TESSA LIVINGSTONE

What inspired the poem?

"Reykjavik Sermon" was inspired by an act of compassion: a veterinarian who got down on the floor, on his hands and knees, to comfort our family dog during her euthanasia. Compassion is really what motivates my work.

What came easiest when writing this poem?

The subjects came easiest: the cows and the dog, the smallness of Reykjavik, the vet who got down on his knees. My dad is a harbor pilot in the Port of Long Beach, so I grew up watching all those big ships come in: oil tankers, container ships, cargo ships—some of which transport livestock. That's where the cows came from: "Consider the container ship, carrying cattle. Pens on the open decks. Their brown eyes, six times too large." Then there was my sister, Molly, who got lost in Reykjavik. It was the middle of the night and she was by herself, just wandering around the harbor looking at all the boats. These were lived experiences, so the subjects were right there. The trick was just synthesizing all that imagery.

What was the hardest part about writing it?

For a long time I really struggled with the form. There were a lot of emotions building through plain-spoken sentiments, so lineation felt like too much of a constraint. I got the idea to call it a sermon since I was working to build a conscious relationship between the physical and the spiritual. The prose form made more sense when I started thinking of it as an oration. Something ceremonial. I'm not interested in a higher power, but I am interested in a higher principle. Jean-Paul Sartre said we should ask ourselves, "What would happen if everyone did what I'm doing?"

What is your favorite line from the poem or the line you are most proud of?

The opening line is my favorite: "Please acknowledge my knocking on." It's a request, not a command. It's a launch pad into another perspective.

Is there anything unique about your personal writing process?

My writing process has been greatly informed by the horror genre. My cousin, who's a visual artist, describes horror as an emotional palette: the film equivalent of a tone painting. Classic horror, in particular, utilizes a full spectrum of emotions: anguish and anxiety, tragedy and despair, grief and hysteria. I practice this same method in my poetry. Although "Reykjavik Sermon" has an overall pensive tone, there are glimpses of the grotesque in descriptions of the dog: "[Consider] the shape of her skull. One side of the skull is never exactly like the other"—and descriptions of the cows, as well: "[Consider] their bodies, to be opened at the throats. Their faces. The flies on their faces." I wouldn't say "Reykjavik Sermon" has the same aesthetics as a horror film, but I'm interested in exploring the same spectrum of emotions. Its center of gravity leans into tragedy, fear, and grief.

How would you personally define poetry?

Franz Kafka, my favorite writer, said it best: "In science one tries to tell people, in such a way as to be understood by everyone, something that no one ever knew before. But in poetry, it's the exact opposite."

What is the best piece of writing advice you've been given?

My poetry mentor, Emily Kendal Frey, told me: "Don't be afraid to name the thing." I've carried that with me ever since.

INTERIORS

MOLLY STURDEVANT

In this poem I argue that although there are legos mixed with old food under the table, an ultrablack fish is scouring the planet at the depth of its drowned bone, jagging puffed sand along the very bottom where no light can. Living fully. You see, for all my knowledge of photosynthesis poultry and Spinoza, I'll still spend this day participating in the slow loosening tumble of things toward lower things. I don't know what you though a poet was. I don't own the means of the loosening tumble. I will always have to decide whether to pull that tiny steering wheel out of the hair and toast or not. That might be as far as I get. One can unload the dishwasher or fold the clothes but not both, not if suddenly teaching elementary school from the corner of a room inaptly named living. Once I was a professional. Once I was a housekeeper. I have congealed to neither now, whence we can safely conclude the end of anthropos, end of polis. I don't know what hedge funds are. I probably won't meet my deductible. I want to hold you and think everything is possible.

INTERVIEW

WITH MOLLY STURDEVANT

What inspired the poem?

The daily grind of being at home during the "high point" of quarantine, while stuck to the computer all day doing remote-learning with my kid, then trying to keep on top of everything else and do my own work in the few evening hours left. I felt like I was forgetting things I knew, losing track of knowledge that was important to me. And I wanted to be able to say something good to my son, about the world, or life, or next year, etc. But it was hard, for the first time really actually difficult, to come up with anything. The poem was sort of exploring that moment.

What was the hardest part about writing it?

It was hard to see it on paper—an admission of how different life had become than what it was or what I'd hoped for. And not just in terms of myself, but in terms of the extent of the changes across the globe.

What came easiest when writing this poem?

The sentences about Spinoza and the deep sea fish. I taught early modern philosophy for a decade at a university. Factual, realistic, or naturalistic images and phrasing come easily and are very grounding for me. It's easy to start there and then build a poem around them.

Is this poem categorical of your work? Why or why not?

Yes. I tend toward writing aphoristic-creative stuff, i.e., prose poems or creative essays. I think it's the influence of the weird, interdisciplinary, pre-strict-genre-era texts of the seventeenth century.

What is your favorite line from the poem or the line you are most proud of?

"I don't own the means of the loosening tumble." I think a lot about this—the precarious nature of trying to maintain middle class or working class existences. The feeling of not having control over things is not just a mere emotional moment—it is a real, economic condition and a source of so much anxiety.

How long have you been writing poetry? What has changed from your first poem to your newest work?

Been writing since junior high. Not even sure what my first poem was. Most recently, I was taught / reminded that there's no need to try to demonstrate intelligence in a poem through sophistic or merely 'clever' articulations. All good poems have an internal wisdom of their own. That was a good thing for me to learn and think about.

Who are some of your favorite poets?

Anne Carson, Billy-Ray Belcourt, Jennifer Moxley, Claudia Rankine, Eve L. Ewing, Joy Harjo, Connie Scozarro, Jake Skeets... so many.

If you had to narrow it down, what three books have had the most impact on your writing?

In the Distance by Hernan Diaz; *Visitation* by Jenny Erpenbeck; *Decreation* by Anne Carson.

Do you work in any other artistic mediums? If so, how do those other genres inform your poetry?

I write in other genres, and I sometimes draw or paint, but mostly it's on the way toward writing something.

What is the best piece of writing advice you've been given?

"Let the reader in."

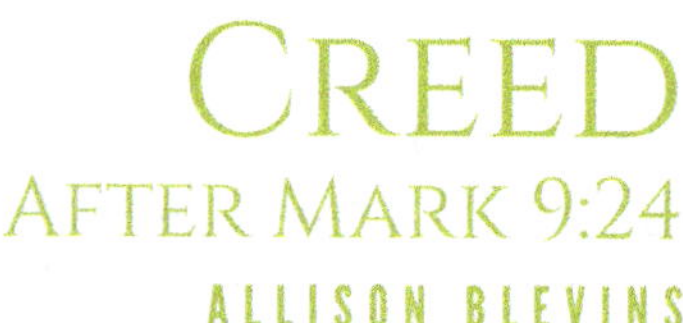

CREED
AFTER MARK 9:24
ALLISON BLEVINS

I believe in the question. The question is a place that breathes bluesmooth. The question breathes from the mouth: lightelectric. I believe in darkness, how the question lives there behind my closed eyelids.

> In every MRI machine, I imagine my body is a coffin. I try to pray but can only remember the Serenity Prayer. I've never been to AA, but *the wisdom to know the difference.* I can feel the contrast metal spread through my body: webbing, bluecream fibers like filament or fringed tendons.

I believe in the machine, in the whir, the yellowswill that thrums and buzzes my bones. I imagine my fillings loosen. I believe my body is the question and creator. Here, in the machine, my body, the question, and you:

> how I love you and how I don't, how we hurry and slow, how we need and the blackblack space between us, in us, and around us. I believe I am small. *Help me overcome my belief.*

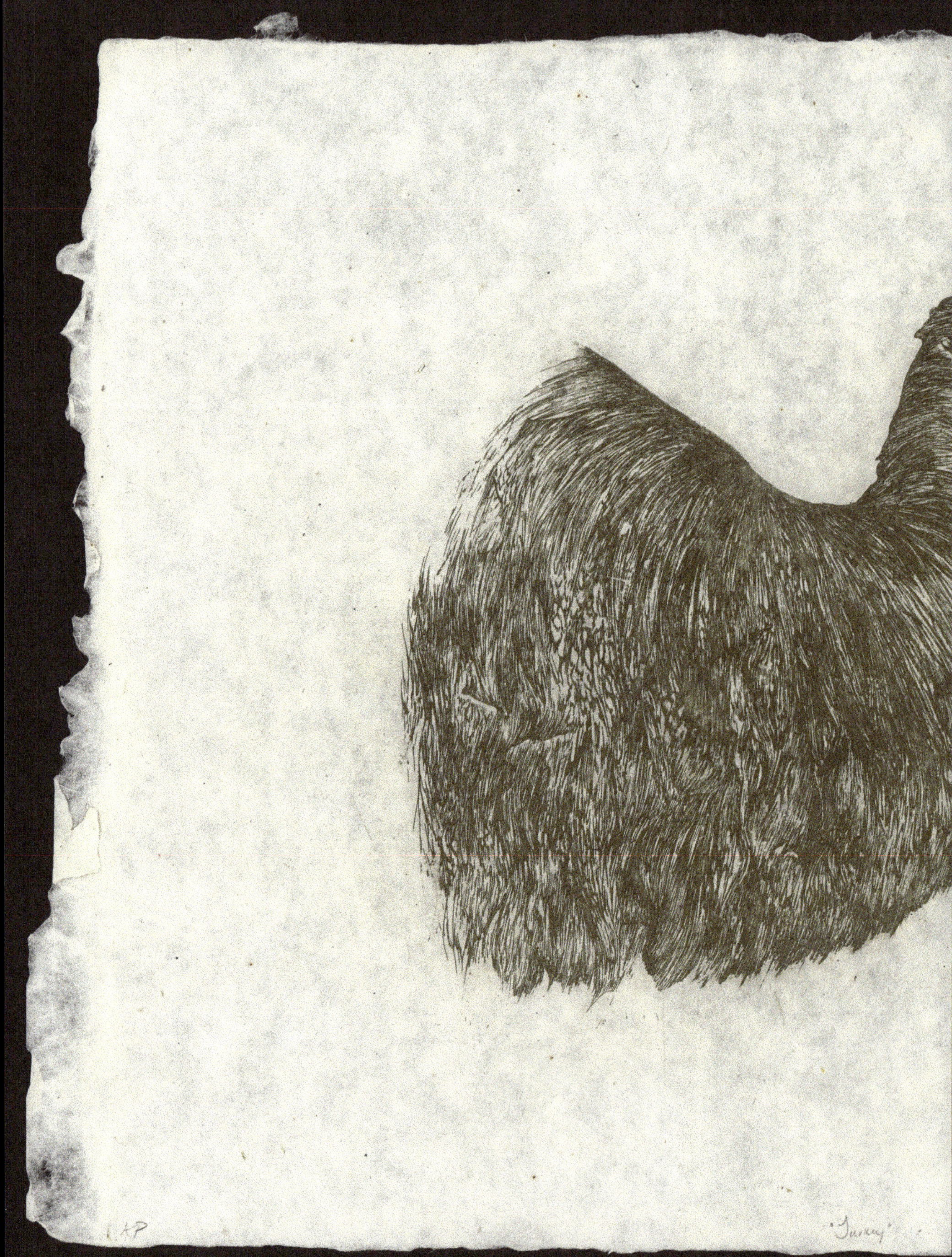
AP
'Turkey'

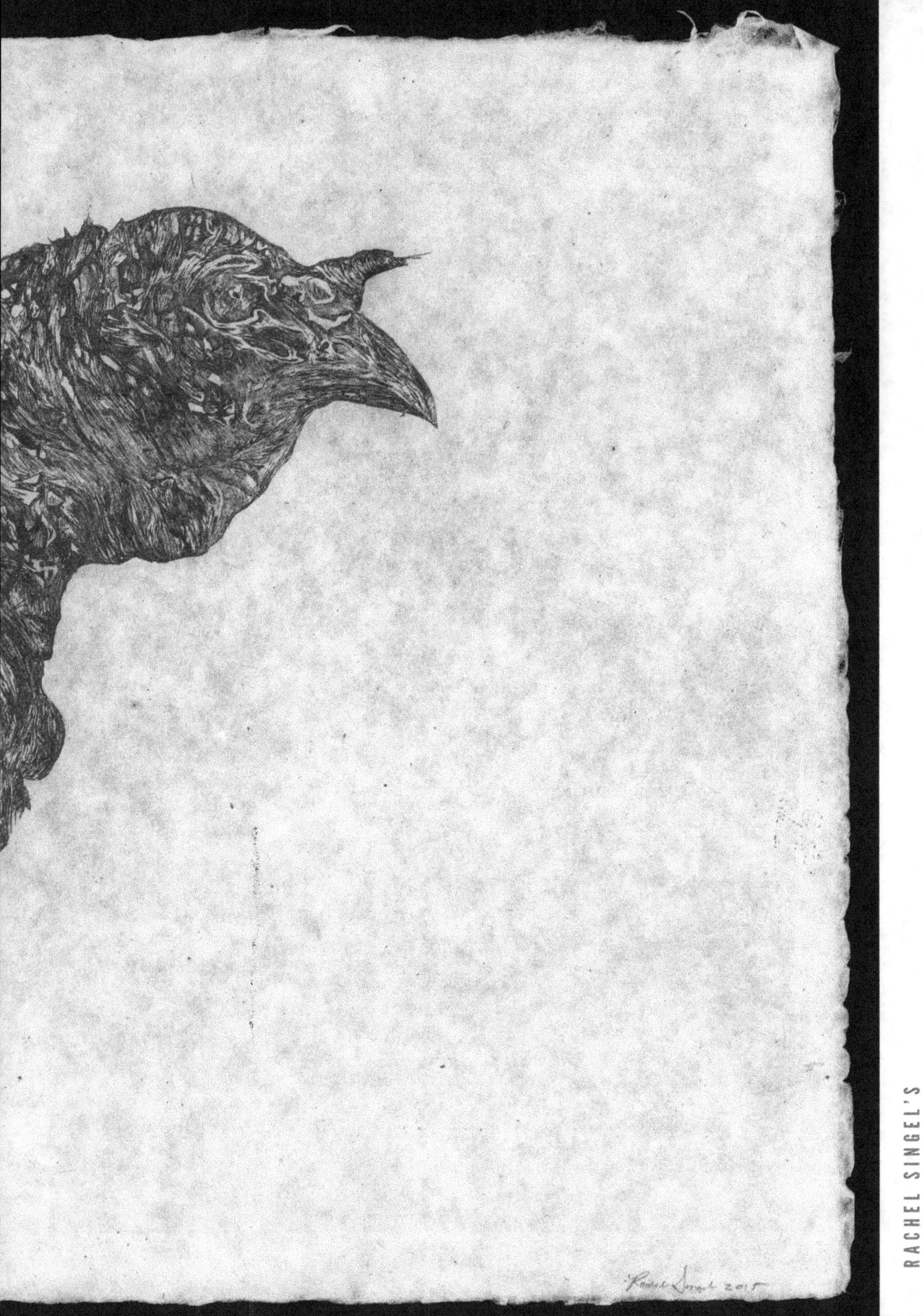
Rachel Singel 2015

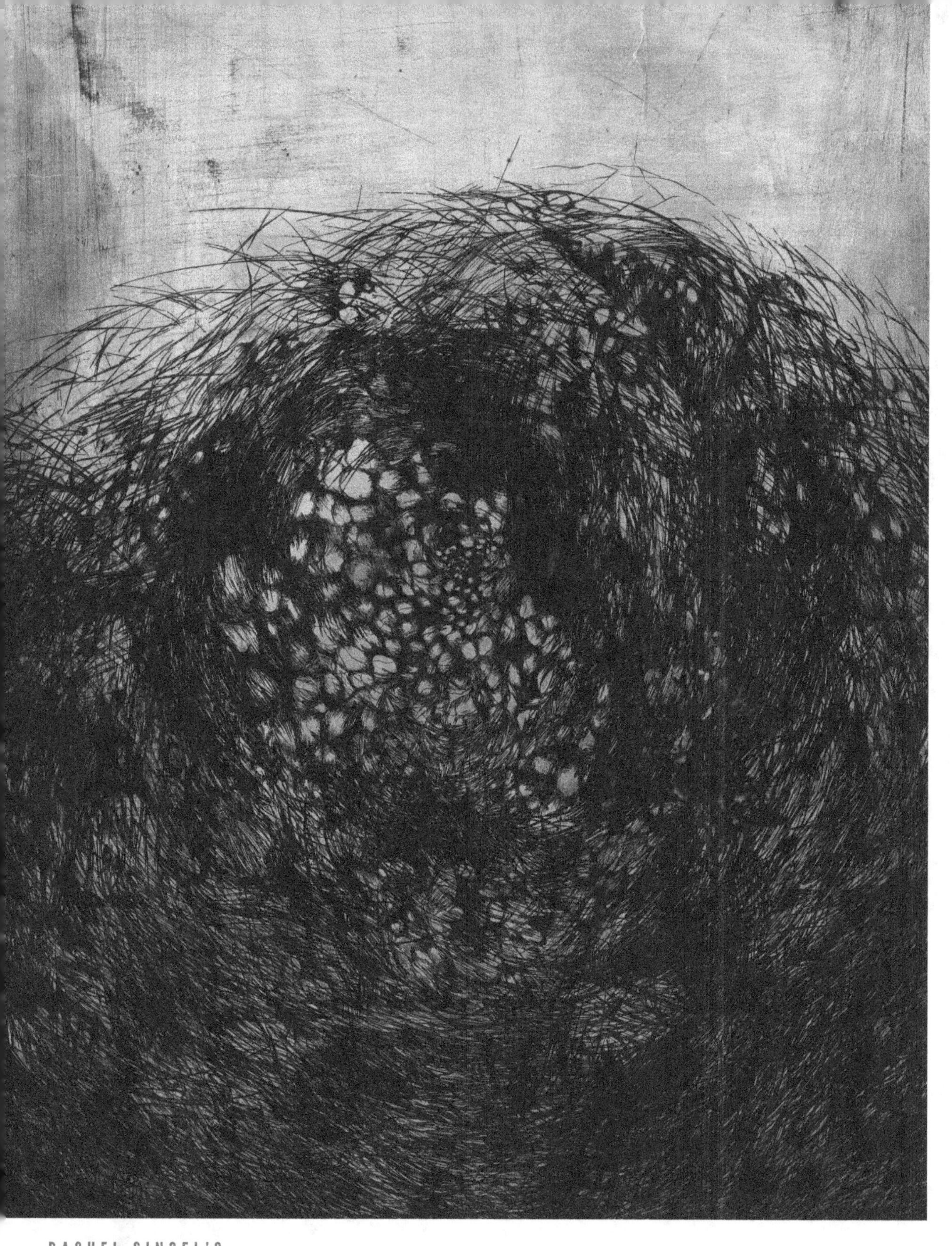

RACHEL SINGEL'S
VENETIAN NEST

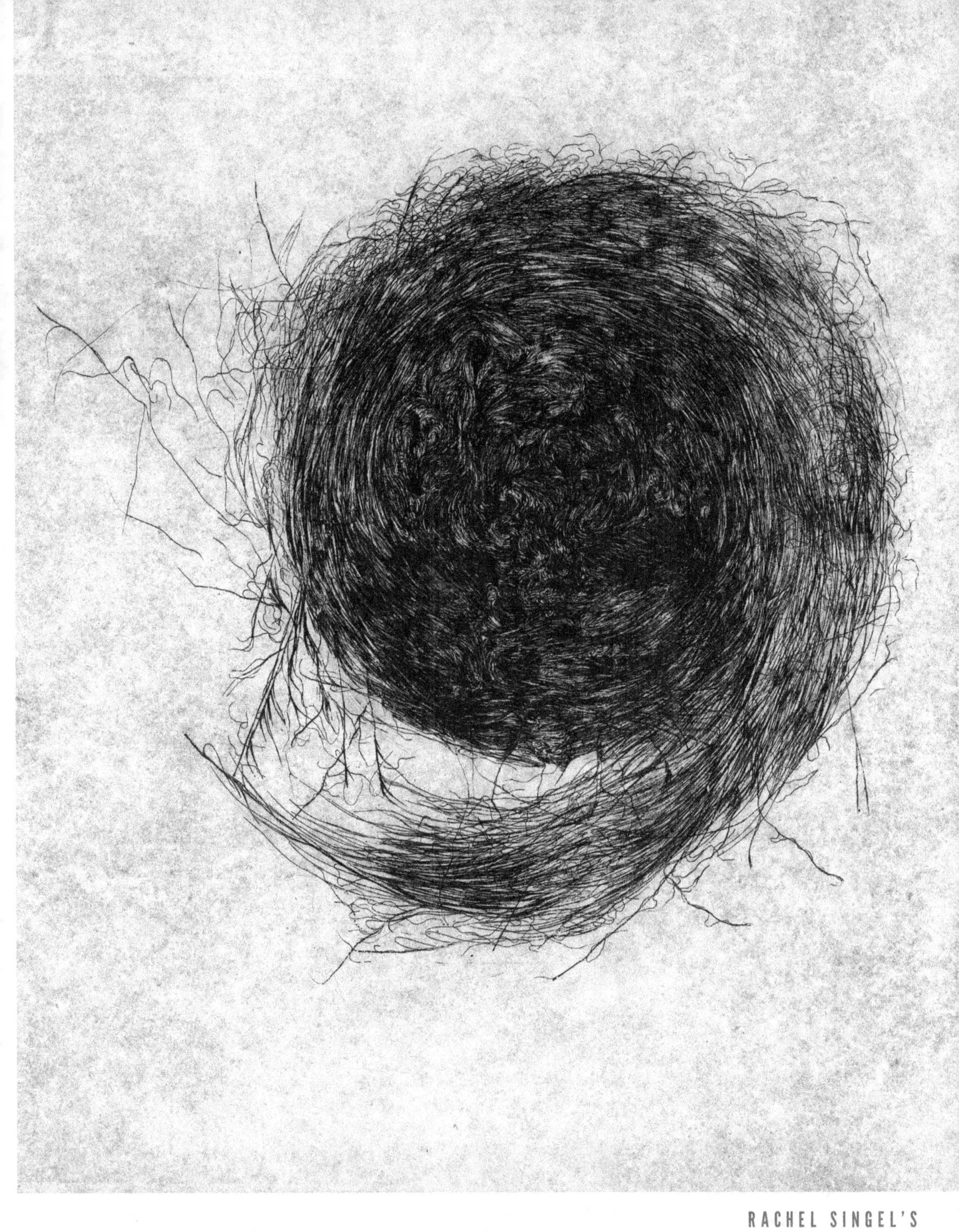

RACHEL SINGEL'S
NEST

RACHEL SINGEL'S
RADIATING TREE

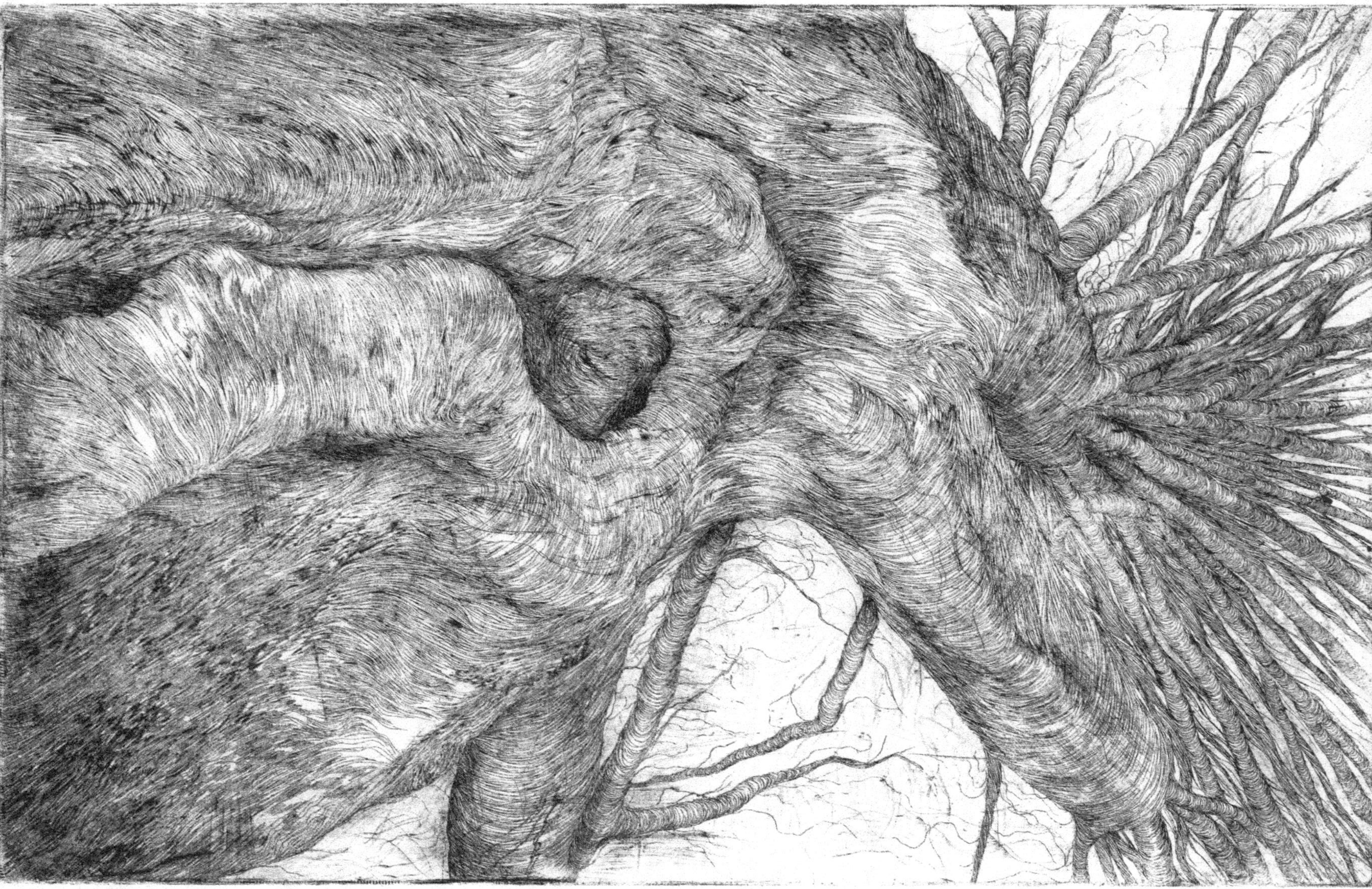

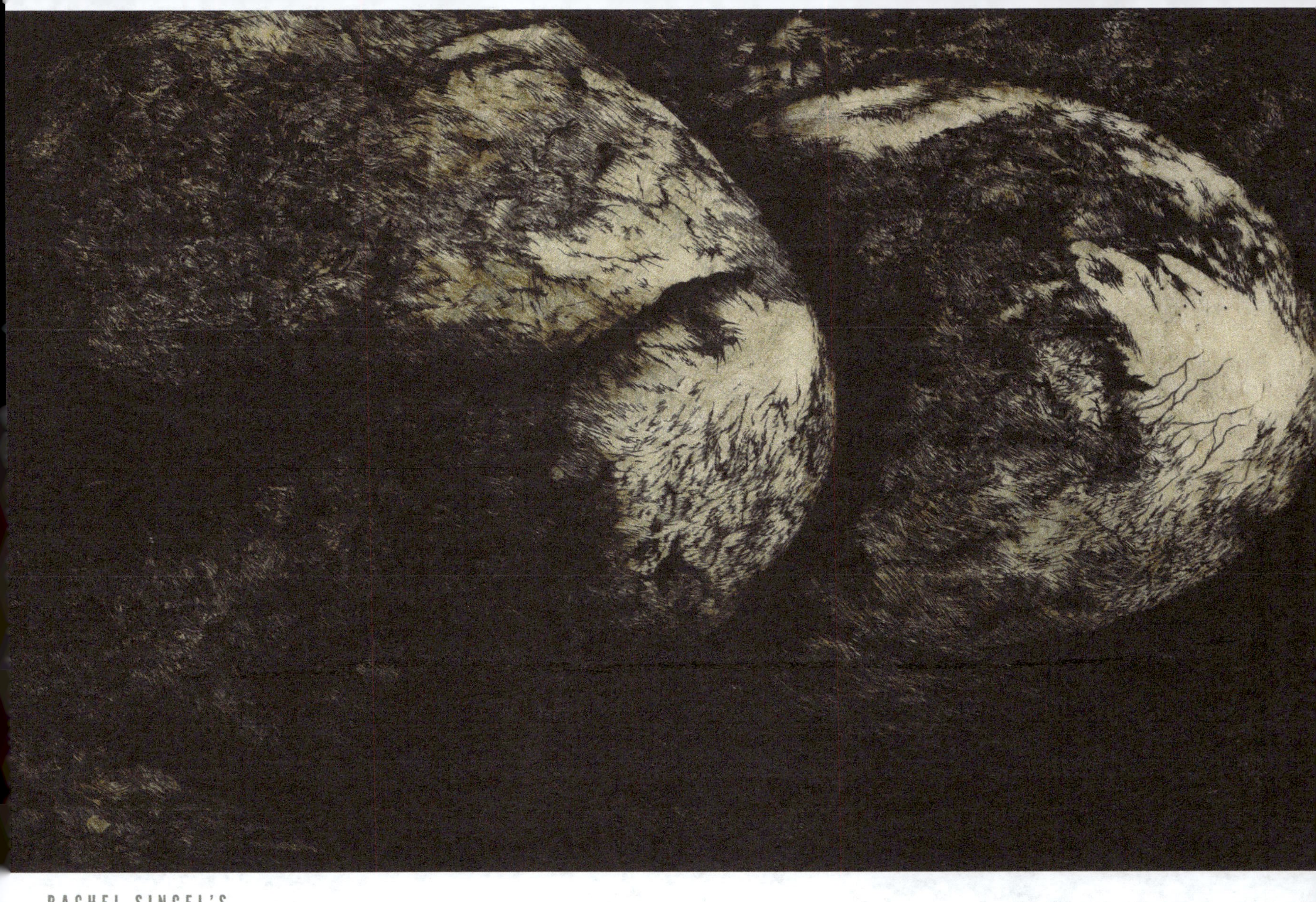

RACHEL SINGEL'S
EGGS

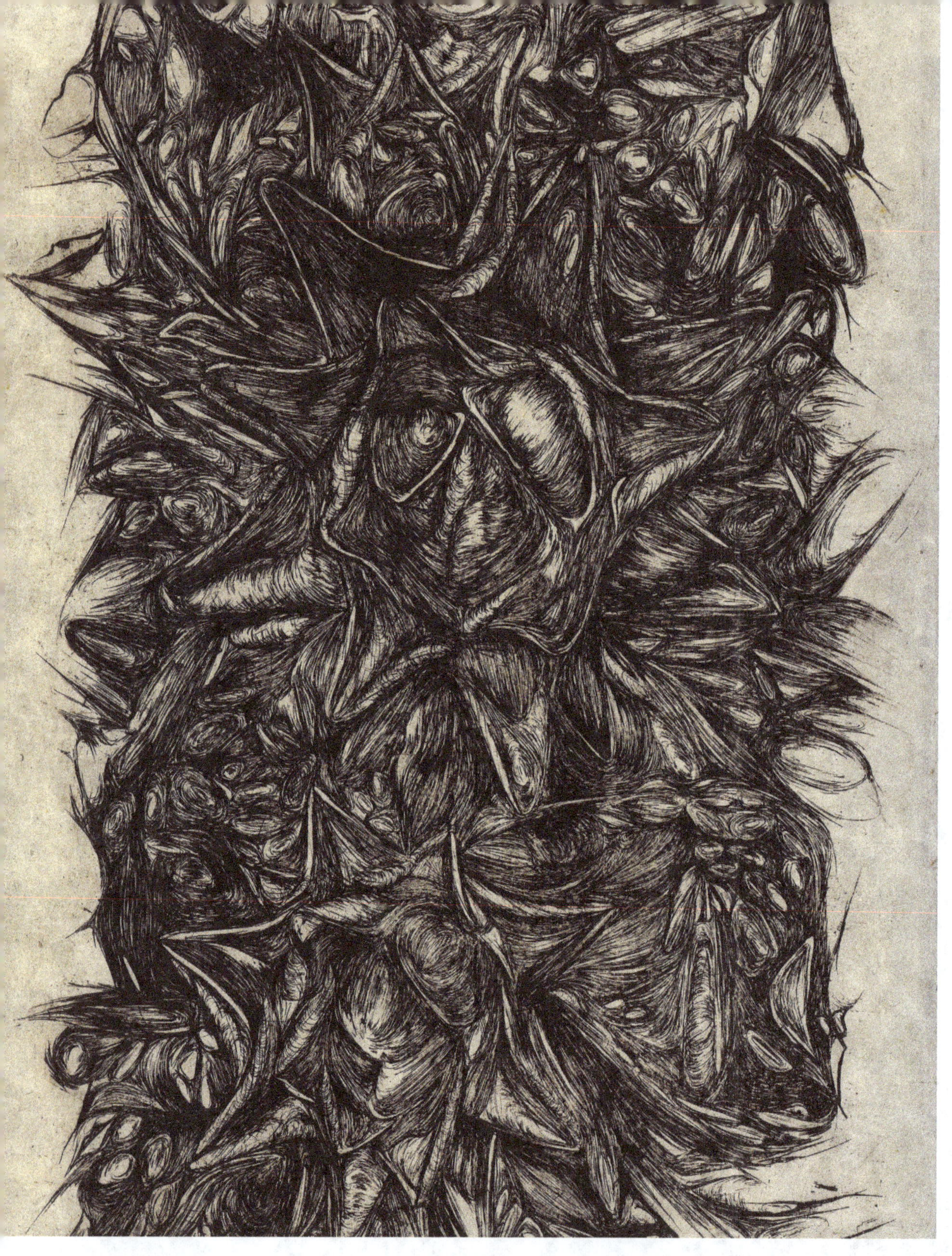

RACHEL SINGEL'S
ARTICHOKES

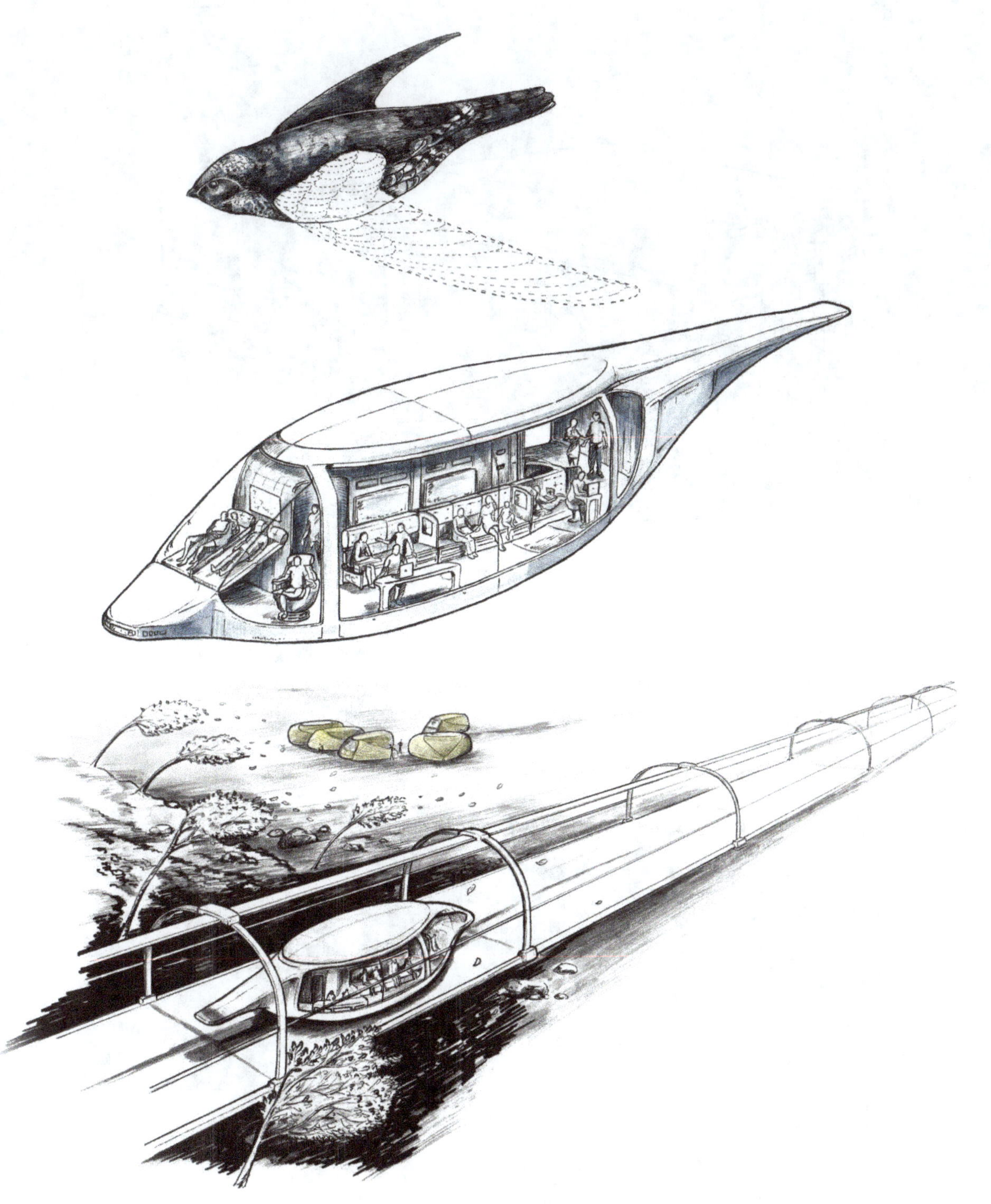

DUSTIN JACOBUS:
BIOMIMICRY: THE SWIFT

DUSTIN JACOBUS'
NOMAD LIFESTYLE

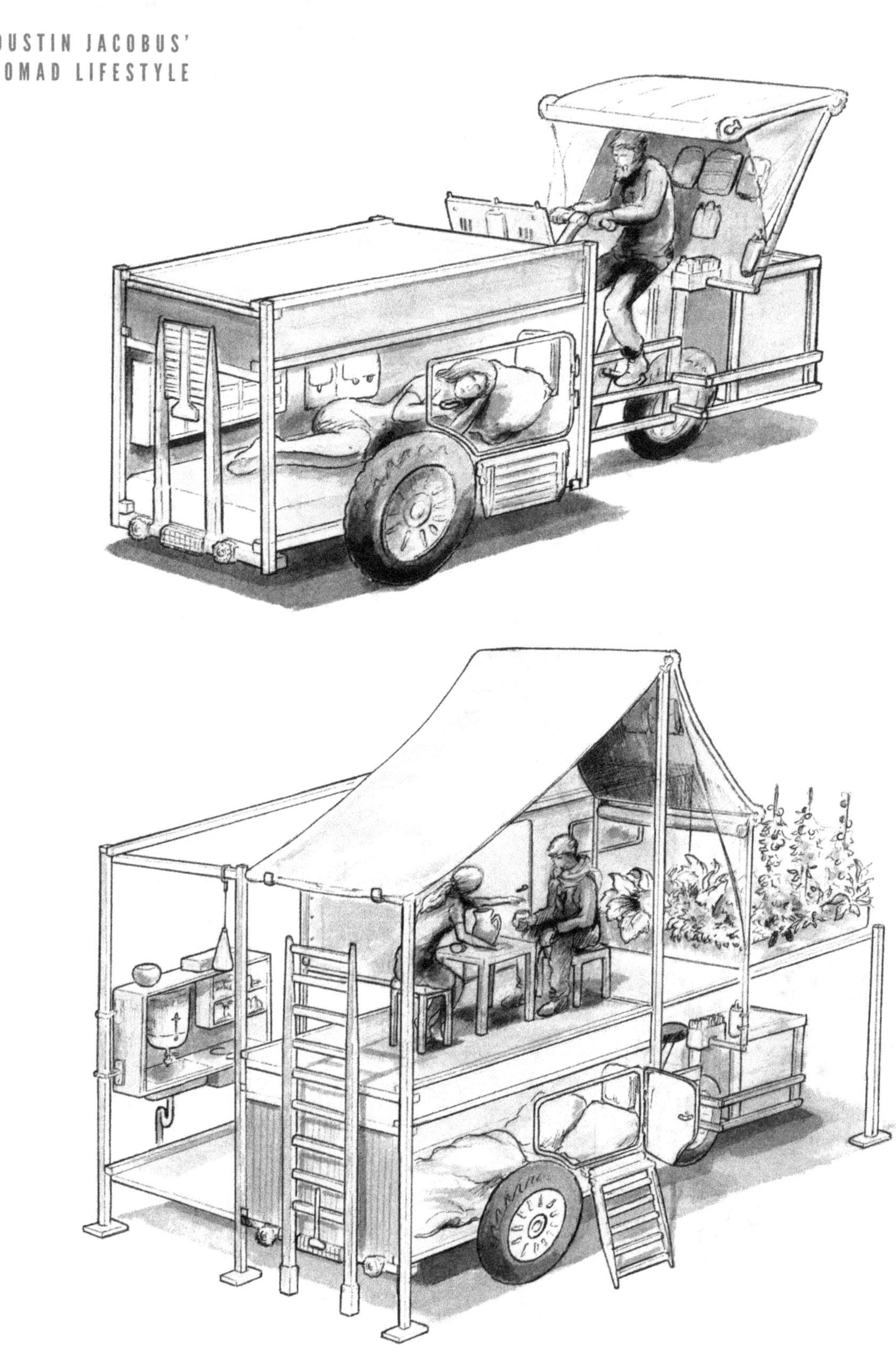

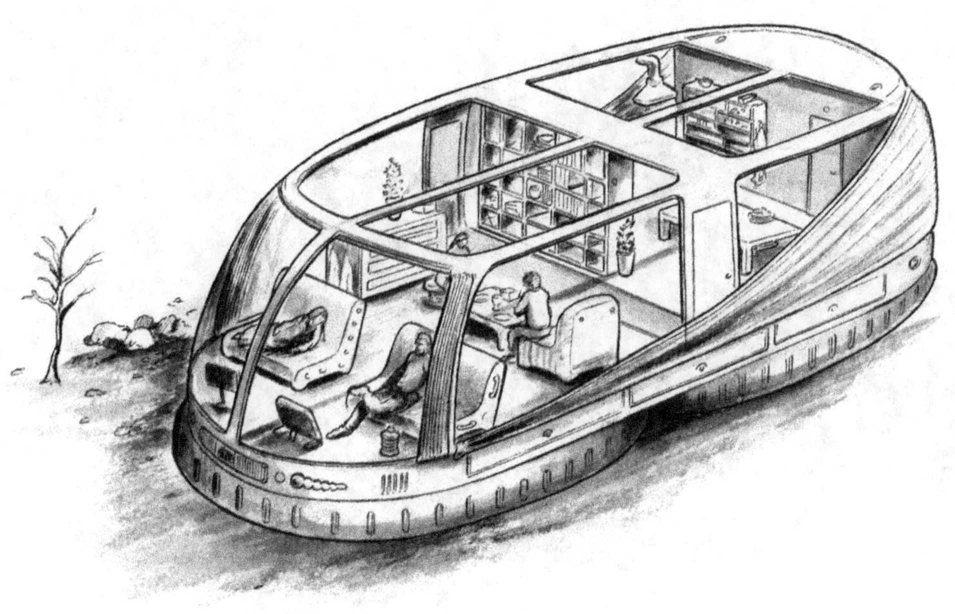

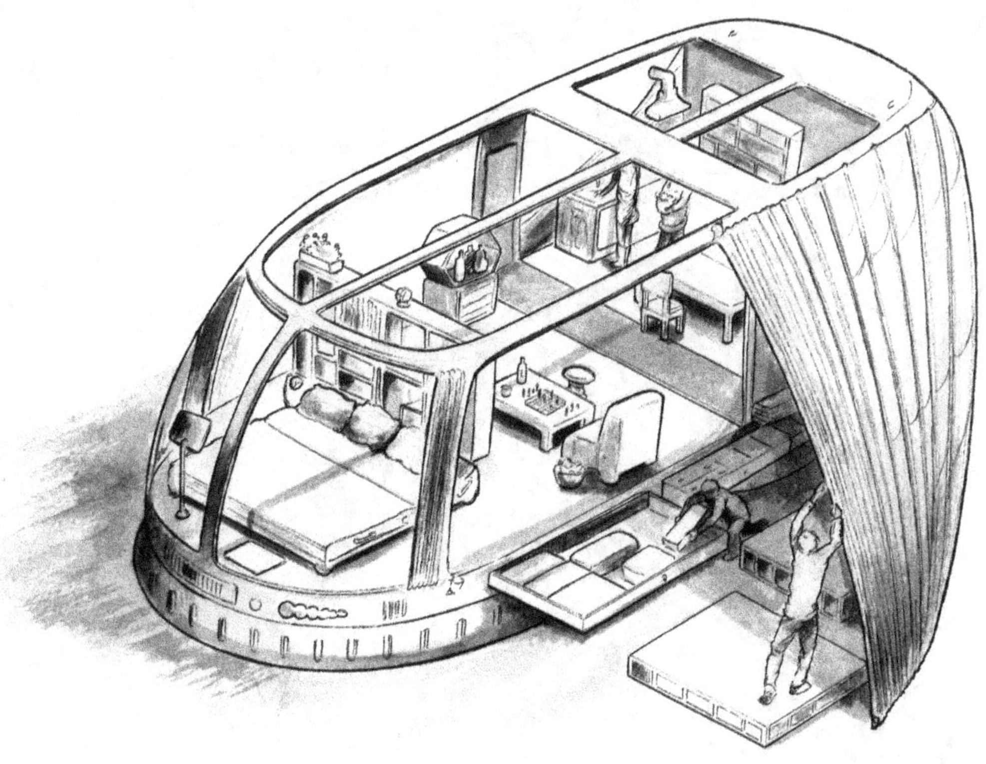

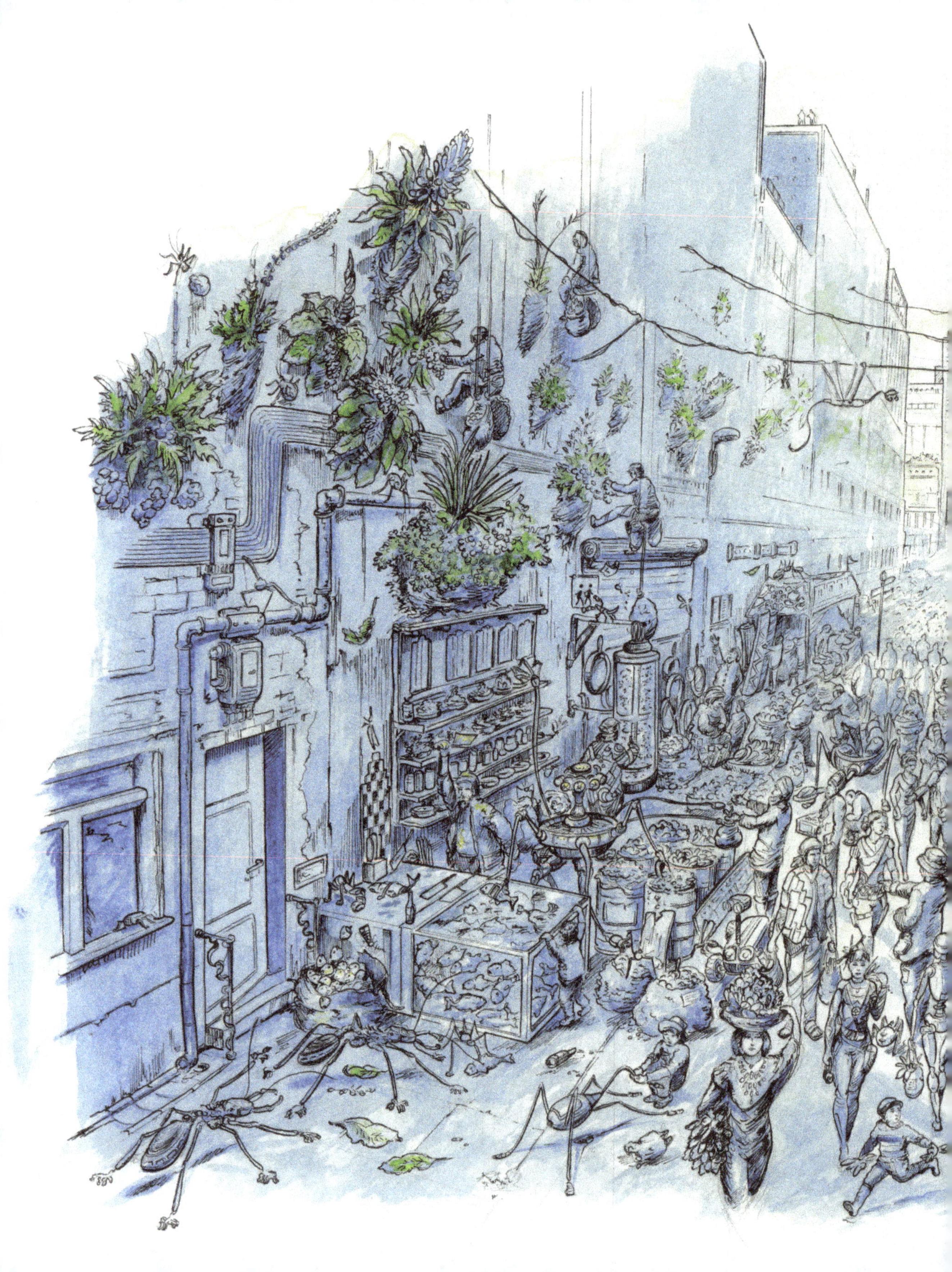

DUSTIN JACOBUS'
CITY SCENE:
ART AVENUE

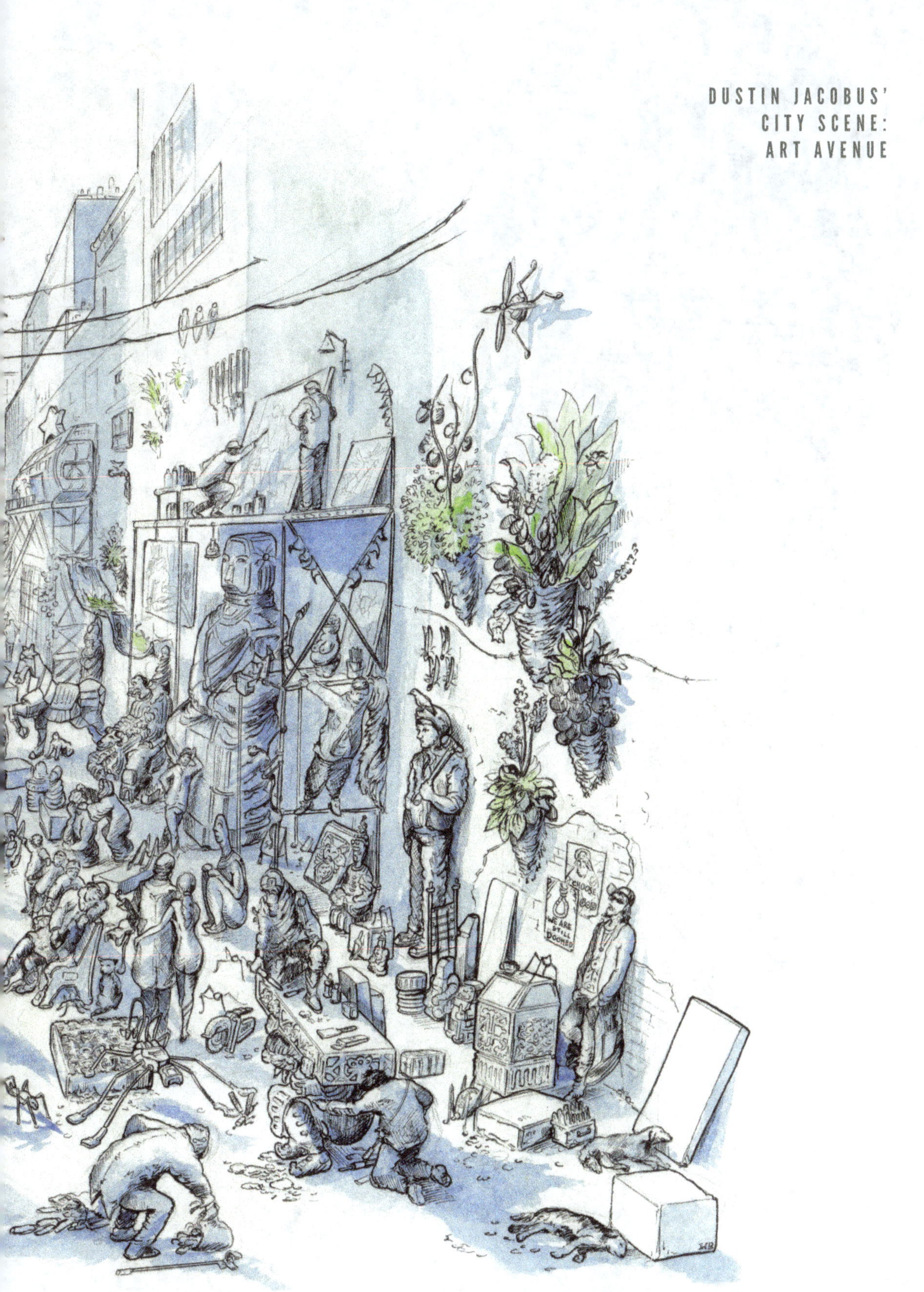

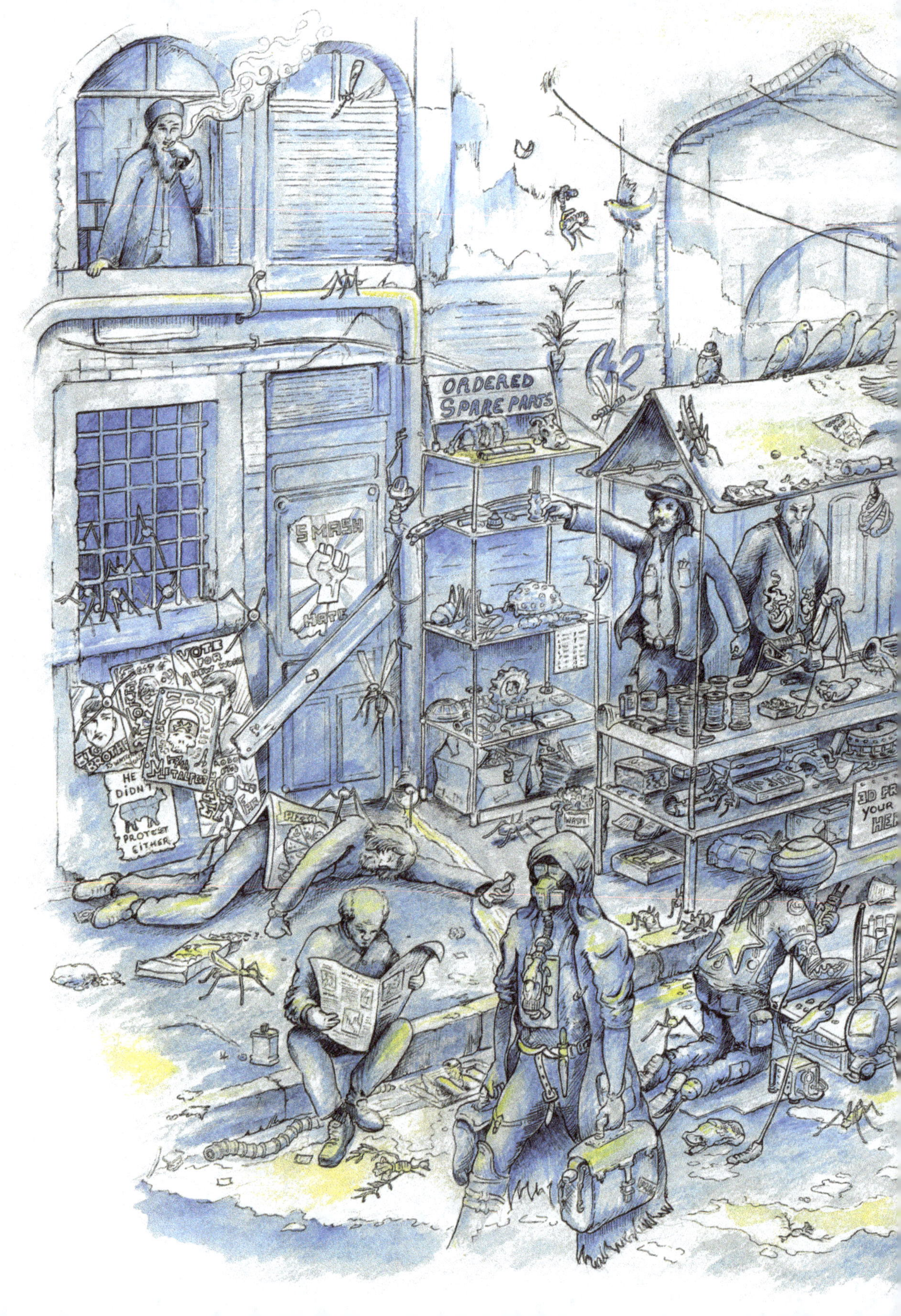
ORDERED SPARE PARTS
SMASH
HATE
VOTE FOR
HE DIDN'T PROTEST EITHER
METALFEST
3D PR YOUR HE

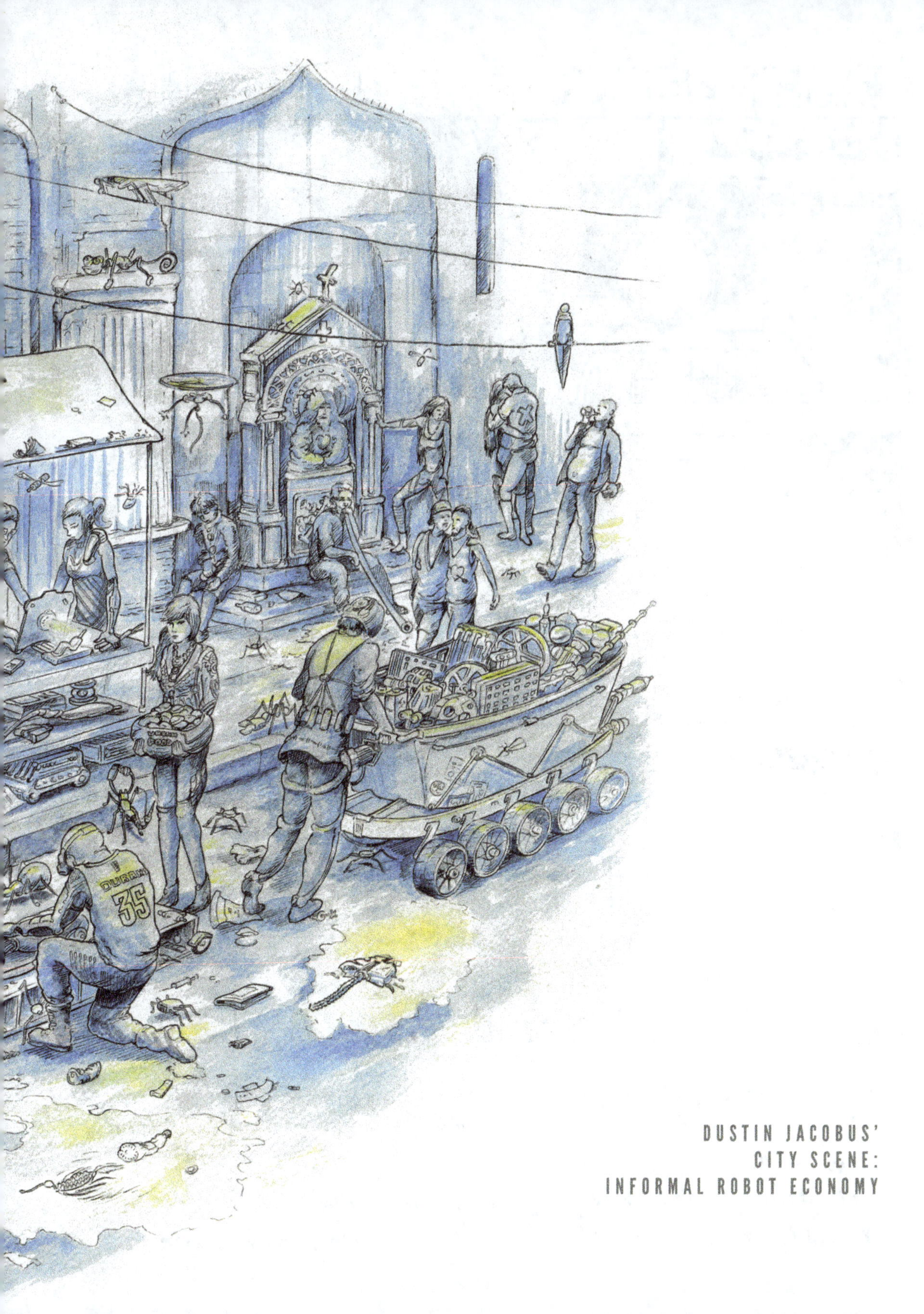

DUSTIN JACOBUS'
CITY SCENE:
INFORMAL ROBOT ECONOMY

EIGHT WEEKS

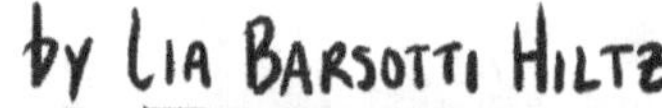

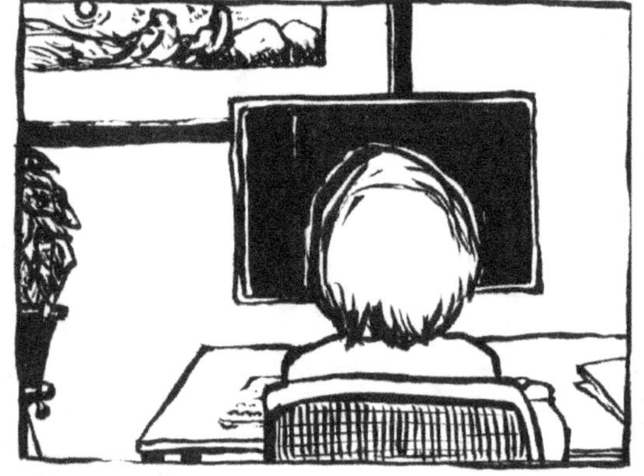

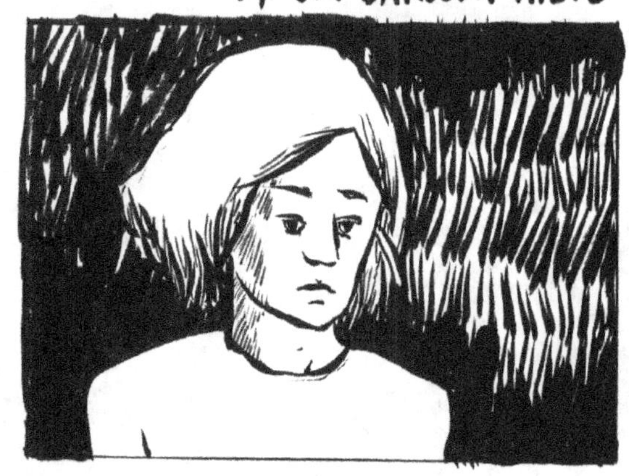

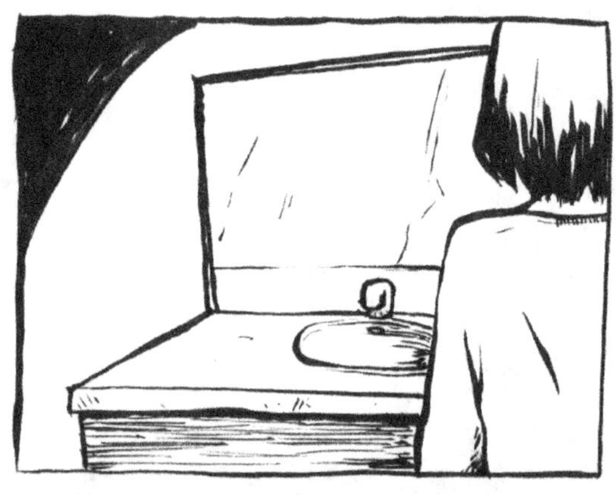

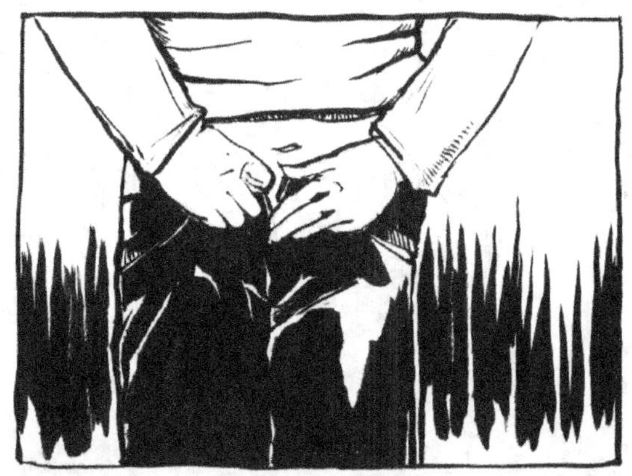

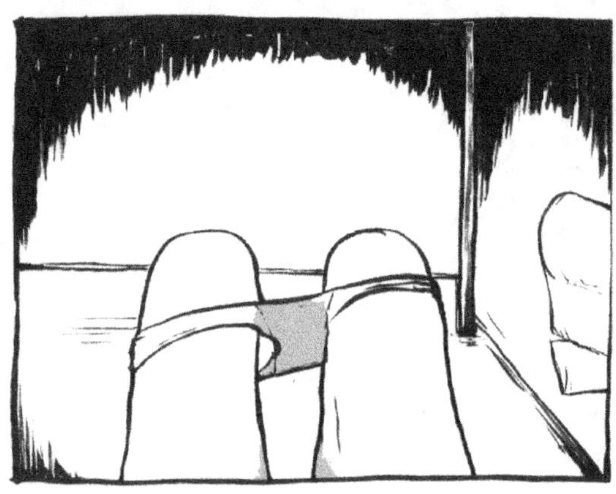

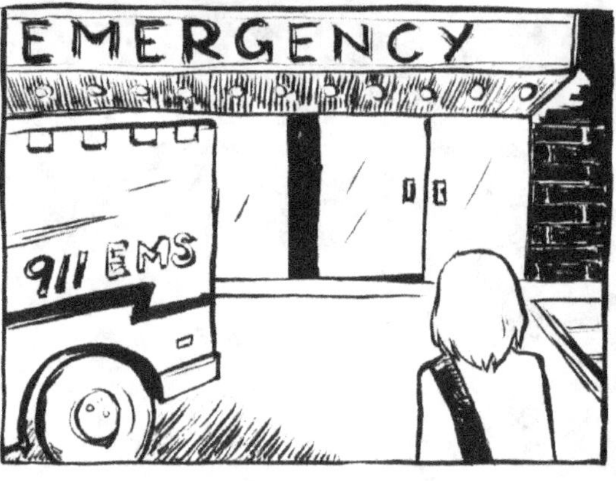

When our second pregnancy came to an end, I drove myself to the hospital, and my husband stayed home with our two-year-old. I knew right away that I was miscarrying, because I had the same feeling I get sometimes when I menstruate, a subtle sensation of wetness on wet - like blinking underwater.

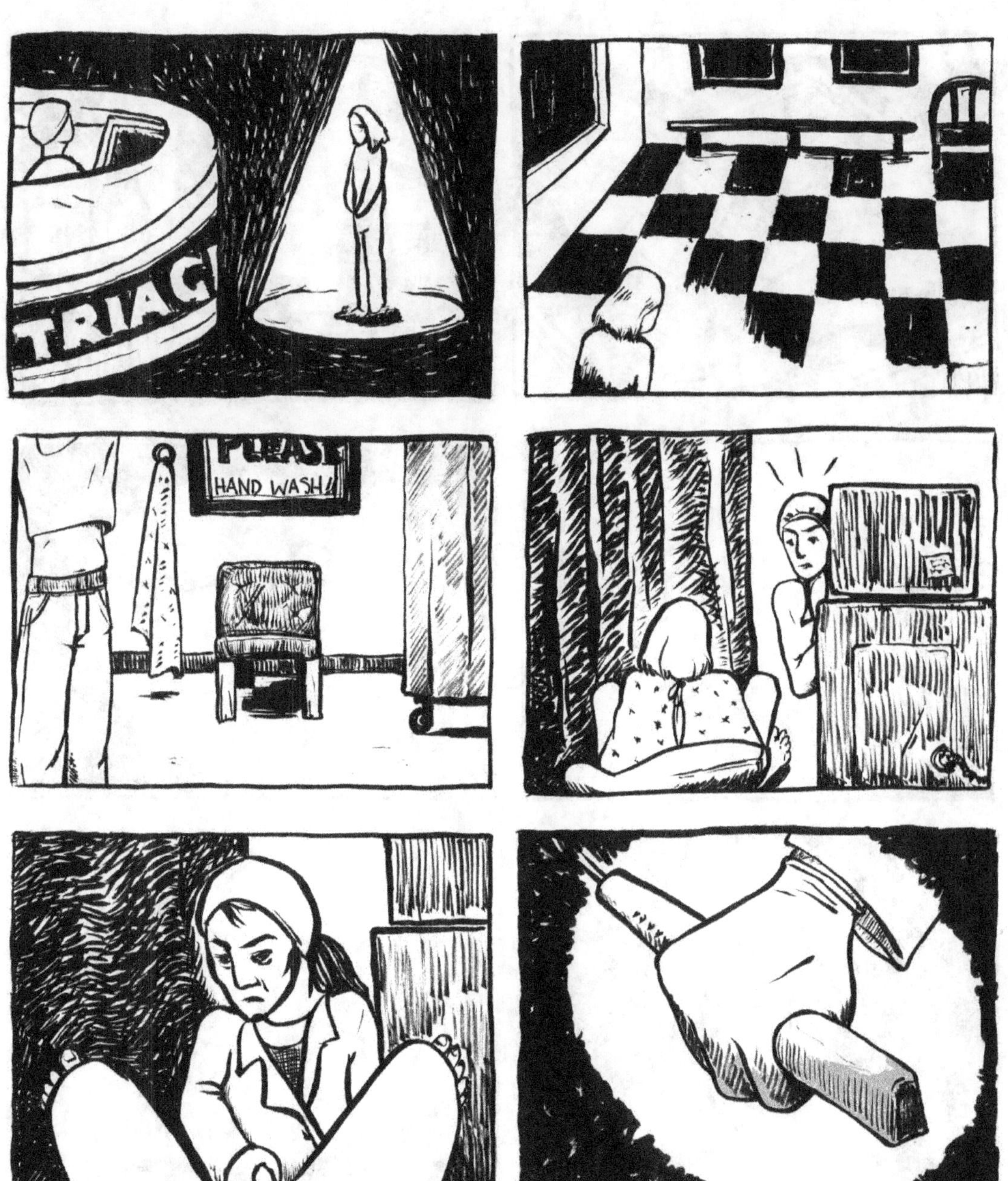

The emergency room was oddly empty. Midweek slowdown, maybe.

I don't know why the ultrasound technician was so uncomfortable. My miscarriage was an ordeal for her, too.

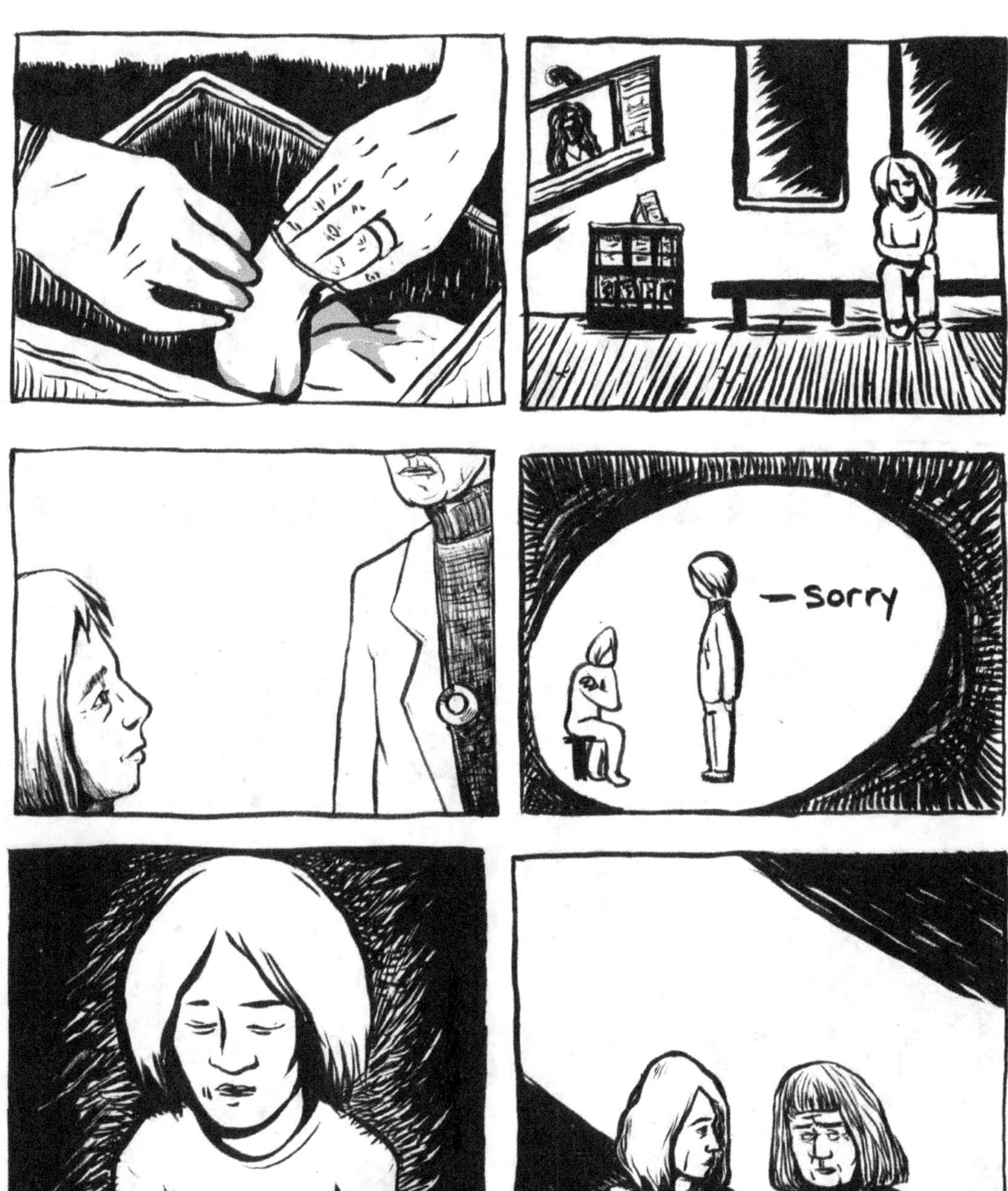

The technician could not interpret the scan for me, so I waited for the doctor. She told me in a gentle way that my baby had died. I knew that already, but it was still hard. It was the first time I heard it out loud.

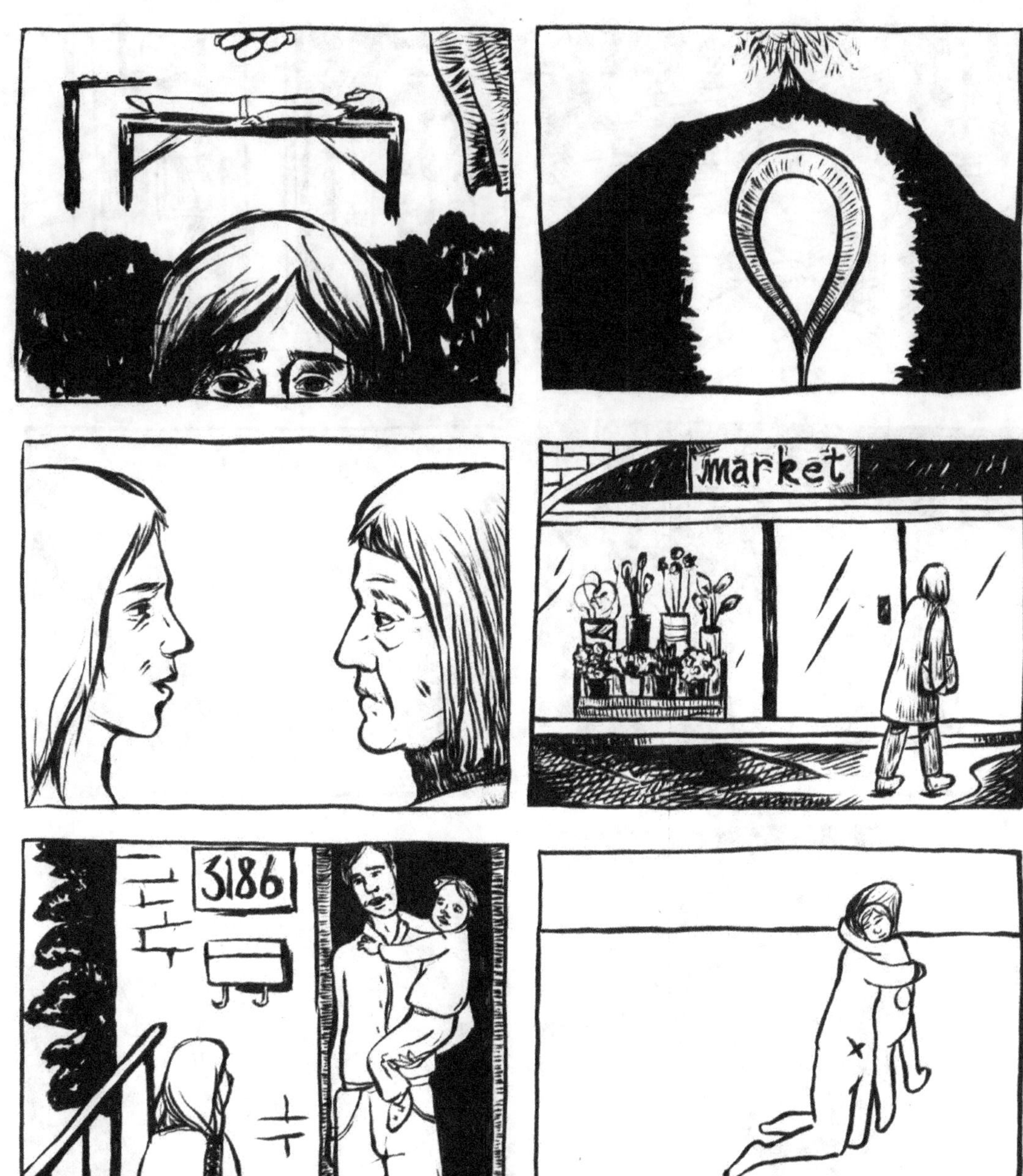

She asked me to decide whether I wanted them to take out the foetus and tissues or if I wanted to wait for everything to pass on its own. She said it could be hours or weeks. Surgery frightens me, so I went home.

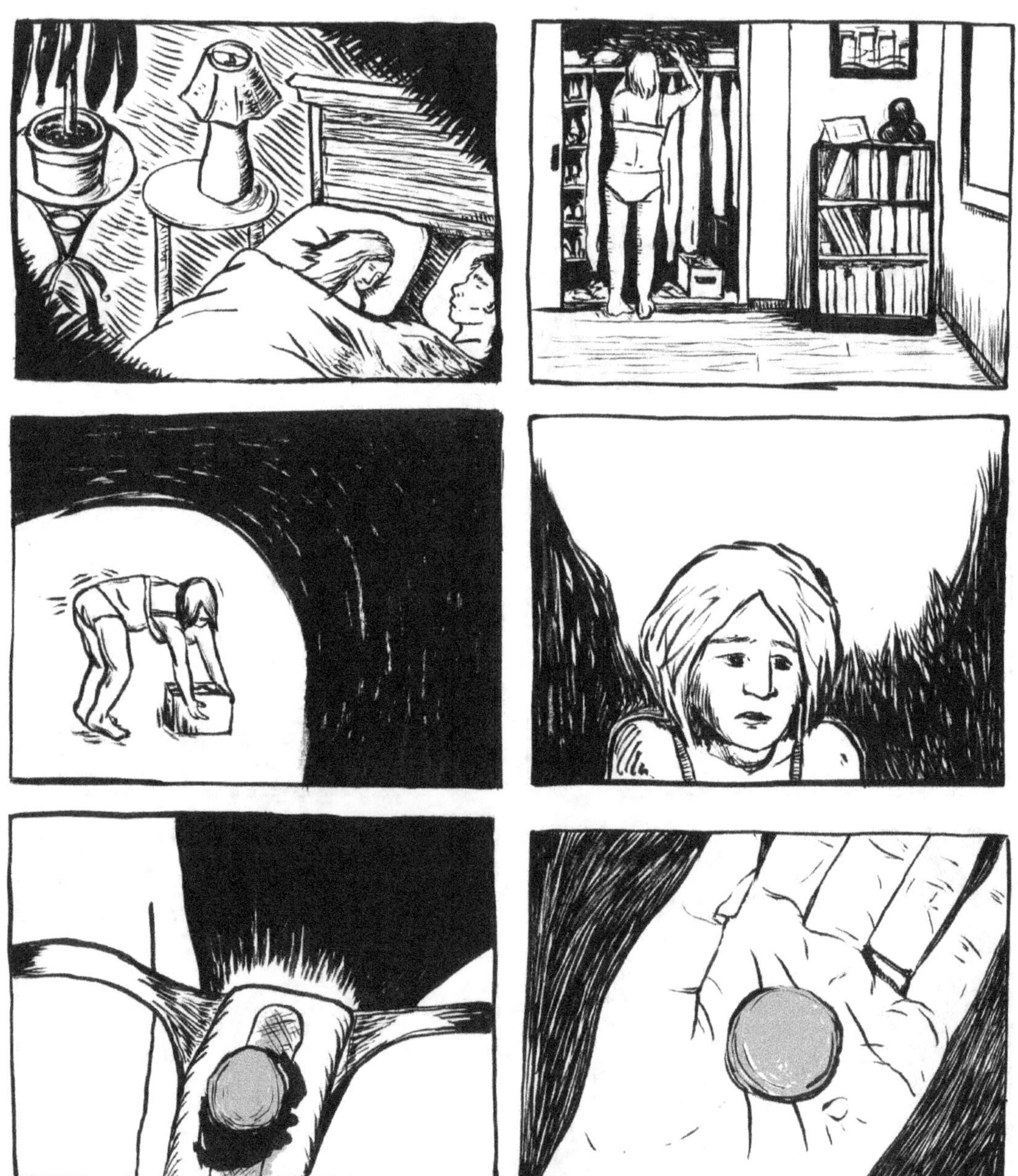

My midwife told me after, that mothers who experience miscarriages perceive them as children who have died. Women who are not mothers, she told me, often see miscarriages as failed pregnancies – reflections of the woman's ability to have children. I do often wonder who my child would have been.

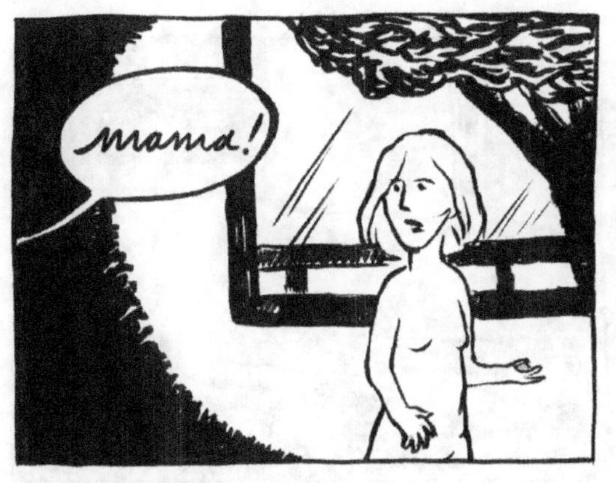

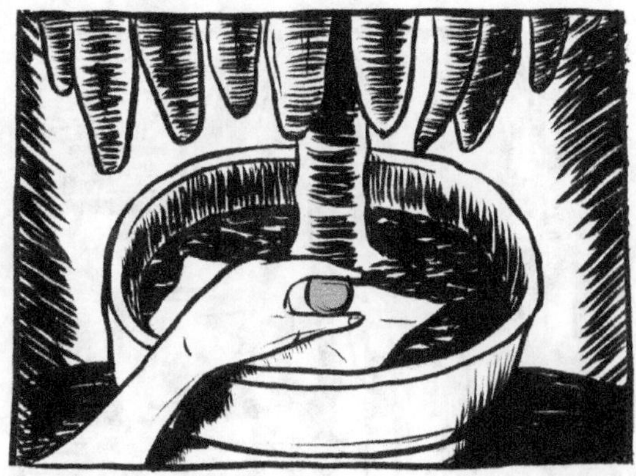
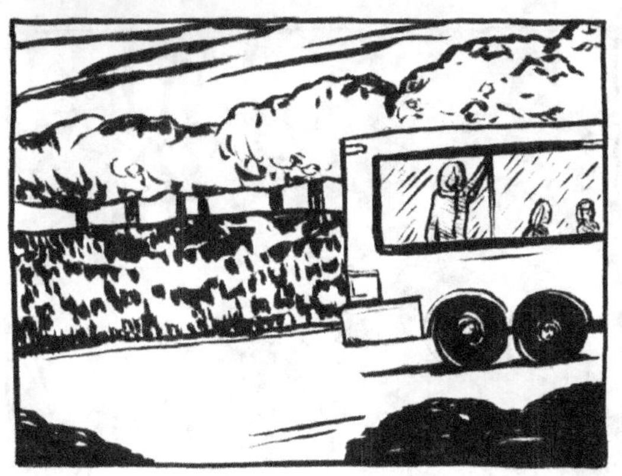
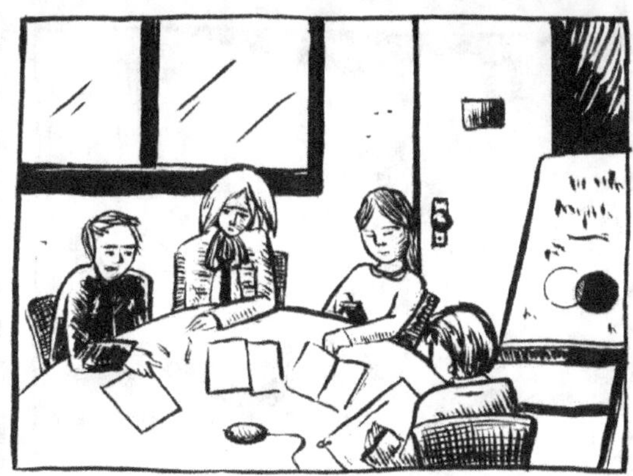
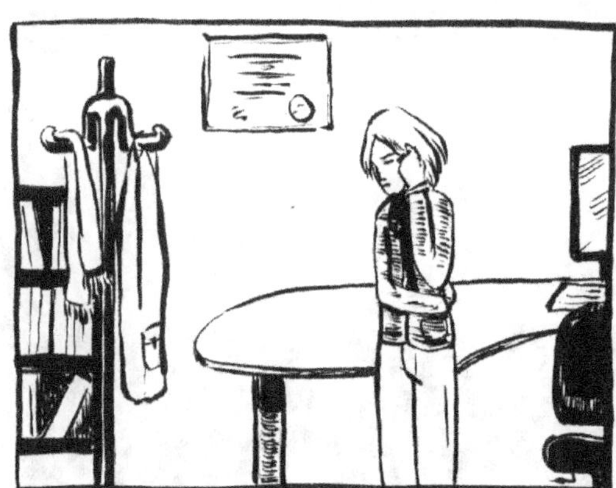
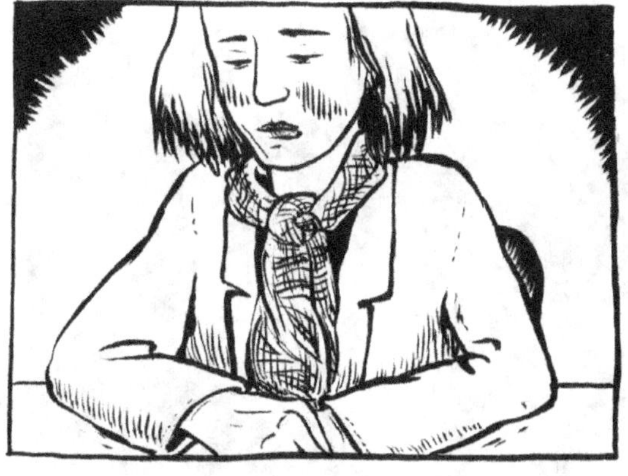

To avoid explaining what I held in my hand to my daughter, I placed it upon a clean tissue on the soil of our bedside plant. I feel defensive about that. But I wanted it to stay with living things.

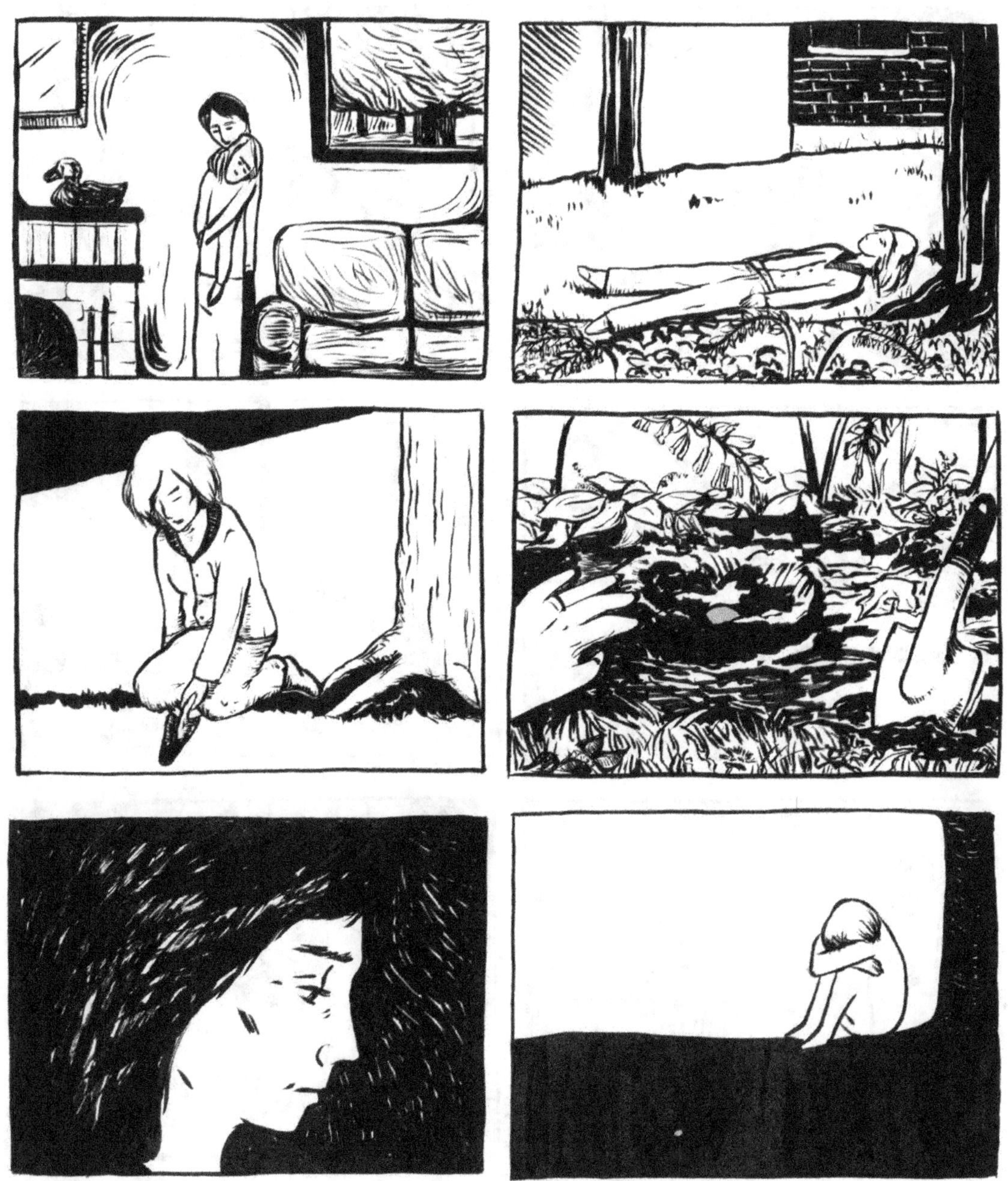

My miscarriage was unexceptional in every way.

We conceived our son later that year.

LH 2020

Interview

with Lia Barsotti Hiltz

What inspired this comic? Tell us more about the origins of its creation and whether any aspects of it were inspired by real life.

I lost a pregnancy in 2011 and, while I took artistic license with the depictions of people, the story is a true one. I was so deep in my emotions at the hospital that I fail to recall people's appearances at all.

What other comic mediums do you work in? Do you have a particular preference?

I am doing a web comic about my neighbourhood in Berlin, and it is just wretched, because it looks like quick little drawings, but actually I probably research and sketch and tool around on my bike for fifteen to thirty hours just to produce one episode. I also am halfway through a graphic novel about a couple dealing with infertility and child loss (it is not as bleak as it sounds). The challenges with it are all about overall structure and planning. I love all my projects, I have to say. I paint, write, etc. I'm really a 'variety is the spice of life' person.

Tell us a little more about the drafting process. What was the hardest part of crafting this comic? What was your planning / outlining process for the comic?

This comic took upwards of two years to complete, with long periods of inactivity. Twice at least I rewrote and redrew it completely. I had never planned it out in the beginning, and "Eight Weeks" started out as roughly forty-eight tiny panels arranged over two pages drawn with a cheap Pelikan fountain pen. I remember cutting the panels out with scissors and rearranging and gluing them endlessly, trying to get the pacing and details just right. It was cluttered and wordless, and unfortunately readers found the story difficult to parse, often coming away with different understandings of the basic facts of the story. Looking back I see that the urgency and emotion were there, but the form was all wrong.

Anyway, this was lost on me at the time. I did not really know what I was doing, let's face it. It is my first real comic with a narrative. So I sent it around, and *Driftwood Press* (thank you!) as well as a medical journal in Canada both rejected it, but they told me that the piece had gone fairly far in their editorial processes. These reactions encouraged me, and eventually I did another version of "Eight Weeks" that was much cleaner, but still the revision failed to solve the basic problems of the thing so, like a lot of artists and writers, I did need to leave the piece on a shelf for a long time in order to get some clarity.

Talk to us a little bit about how you landed on the form your comic takes: six panels each page, followed by narration at the bottom.

When I pulled it out again, I was about to fly somewhere—I forget where now. I remember taking it with me on the flight and inking it with a Pentel Brush Pen on Leichturm paper: it was so easy, the new style came together all by itself, like the proverbial sculpture just waiting to be carved from the rock. I think I only had to redraw one or two panels. I added a bit of air to the story by drawing the panels much larger, moving from two pages in total to a longer form. I thought this would allow the reader to move more slowly.

What parts of this story were the hardest to draft, both narratively and visually? What instruments did you use here?

It took about two years or so from when I first made this thing before I finally gave into the fact that the comic could not remain wordless. The crux is the conversation between the doctor and the protagonist. Without using guiding instruments like a flow chart or other infographic tools, it was impossible for me to get across to the reader that the protagonist must choose between having the fetus removed by the hospital, or waiting for it to pass naturally. As this is the most important moment in the comic for me, the moment where a person can somewhat influence how a difficult experience will end, I needed this to be clear. It's no good when readers are closely examining your artwork just trying to figure out what the heck is going on, you know what I mean?

Just to back up, I had excluded text originally from the comic for a reason. Most people know me as a highly verbal person. I talk to myself out loud even when I am alone. Yet, certain experiences—this miscarriage, giving birth, breastfeeding, physical intimacy with my kids—are so full of meaning and communication in such a way that verbalising can feel either shallow or shocking. Just, the wrong part of the brain. Again, I am just talking about my own perceptions and feelings. This is not universal. And I find that when text is in a comic, readers zero in on it immediately. Text usually wins.

So I took a whole bunch of graphic novels off my shelves and explored all the ways I had seen artists include written language in comics. I saw that there is a clear difference between comics that include speech and thought bubbles within the panel, and comics that keep a clear delineation between speech and image. The latter method held promise for conveying the silence I was looking for, while also allowing me to do some exposition. I wrote the texts using the past tense so that the reader would take the text as reflections made at a later time. This way, when looking at the images, readers remained undistracted by text. My text illustrates the images, not the other (much more common) way around.

You opted to handwrite the words rather than use a font. What do you think this adds to the intimacy of the writing?

I handwrote the words in Photoshop, while the art was done traditionally on paper using a brush pen. Handwriting allows me to match the art better, its line thickness, colour, etc, unlike fonts in font packs. This harmony in the overall look and feel of the work feels very important because the risk of keeping the text separate from the panels is that it feels like two pieces of creative work badly jammed together. The handwriting keeps it harmonious.

Perhaps the most shocking line was one of the final lines: "My miscarriage was unexceptional in every way." This line really drives home the theme of the work. Would you like to discuss that line in more detail?

Miscarriage is really banal. I wanted the writing to reflect how things like this occur in the everyday. Some emotional moments, like weddings, grad ceremonies, funerals, they get set aside from regular life with ritual and ceremony. Whether we like their formats or not, those ceremonies give us a path to follow with our feelings as well as formal acknowledgment. But other things happen to us only privately.

I remember realising many years ago that a beloved man no longer loved me back. I had to wrap up my life with him and move on without a songbook for it. Unrequited love is as normal and mundane as it gets, but it still hurts, you still have to go through the difficult emotions as well as the practical matters as best you can, the grieving and the recovering. Similarly, the miscarriage depicted in this story happened to me in a totally normal time and a totally normal way. There are other totally normal ways to have a miscarriage, but this was mine. I still had to go through it, feel it, and move on. Isn't it true that the greatest peaks and valleys of our lives are also incredibly normal, for all of their power?

I feel also that creative works today do not provide enough explorations of moving through life's many highs and lows thoughtfully, fully, healthfully. We are a long ways away from the didacticism of Victorian english writing. Now, we are very good at chronicling trauma, on the other hand. Looking back on this piece in the context of my other creative work, I realise a central theme for me is resilience.

What are the challenges of writing about intimate family moments?

The greatest difficulty with memoir is discretion and the greatest difficulty with intimate family moments is misunderstanding. I cannot count all the things I would like to make art about that I have always avoided, because I know the people involved would feel injured just seeing themselves represented in my art.

As for misunderstanding, I find that everything is political nowadays, and that artworks with no political agenda can be exploited to prove something to someone. For example, just by making art about miscarriage I have maybe inadvertently contributed to the conversations about what topics are valid for art-making, what topics should women artists address, how "should" women behave during a miscarriage, do hospitals handle women properly, and so on. But my work is not polemic disguised as art.

How would you describe your aesthetic? The thick line work in this comic creates stark visual moments throughout this harrowing story. Is this style indicative of your work as a whole, or does this comic feel unique visually?

This style is one of several and, in fact, I struggle with the basic market requirement that artists produce consistent work so that clients and book-buyers know what they are getting. While I understand this, it is stultifying for me creatively, and I personally wish that readers would be open to works using multiple styles. We see this in manga, and I wish it would take root in western comics, too. I dream of making works that flow seamlessly from one look to another, according to what would work best in each part of a story. I spend too much time forcing myself to make consistent work.

Transitioning from creating artwork to fully-fledged comics can often feel daunting for artists. Do you have any tips for aspiring comic writers? What were things you wish you would have known when you were starting out?

No, I have no tips. I only started out a few years ago, and would welcome some mentoring myself! But in all seriousness, I did start this comic thing after decades of office work, and I have been very pleasantly surprised to see how many skills transfer from my old life to this one. I had tried after university to "be" an artist, but gave up. Looking back, I see that I had talent and lots of artistic development, but not the slightest idea how to put together a career, a business plan, a project, nothing. I learned all that in another industry, and finally now can handle the many, many, too many administrative, financial, communications, marketing, etc. tasks of doing artistic work. Also, I just am not that ambitious anymore, and that really really helps me focus on the work itself. I would recommend Lynda Barry's book *What It Is* to all beginners, because it helps one get in the right frame of mind artistically. The second piece of essential reading is Kriota Willberg's *Draw Stronger*, because if a person wants to spend hours hunched over a desk with their hand clutching a pencil, they need to do it carefully. Chronic injuries are a plague in the comics community.

If you had to narrow it down, who would you say are your three biggest influences?

Alison Bechdel, absolutely. *Are You My Mother?* set an impossibly high bar both artistically and intellectually. But long before I saw her work, I was exposed to David Mack. Sadly, seeing his work decades ago gave me the impression that his effortless style-crossing and creativity were common in comics. It is not common anywhere! He is just a wonderful artist, and I pull open his *Kabuki* books often simply to be reminded of what is possible. Birgit Weyhe is my inspiration when it comes to chronicling people. She is a master of tone, tact, and pacing. Sadly, to my knowledge her work is not available in English.

STRATEGIES of BEING

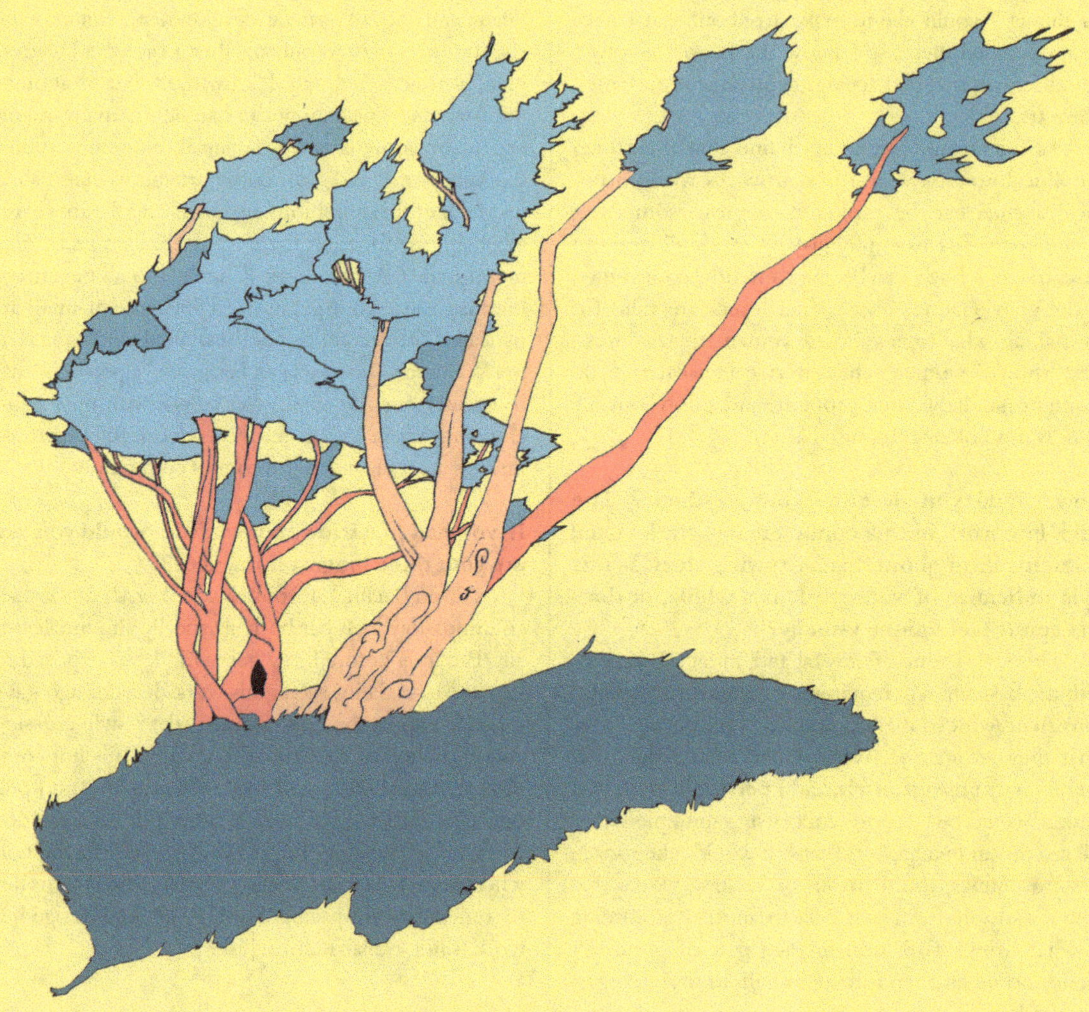

ILLUSTRATIONS FOR AN UNWRITTEN ESSAY

by COCO PICARD

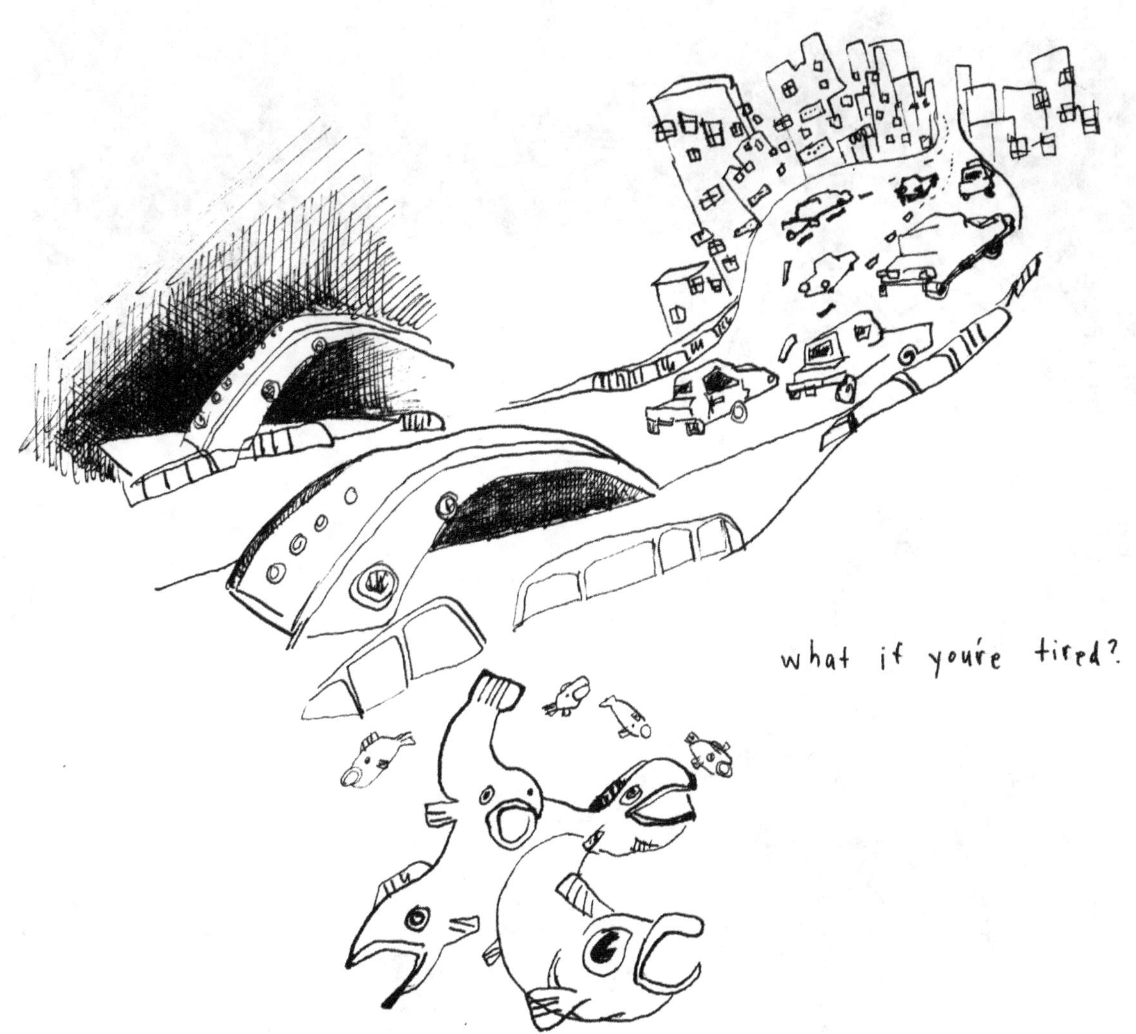
what if you're tired?

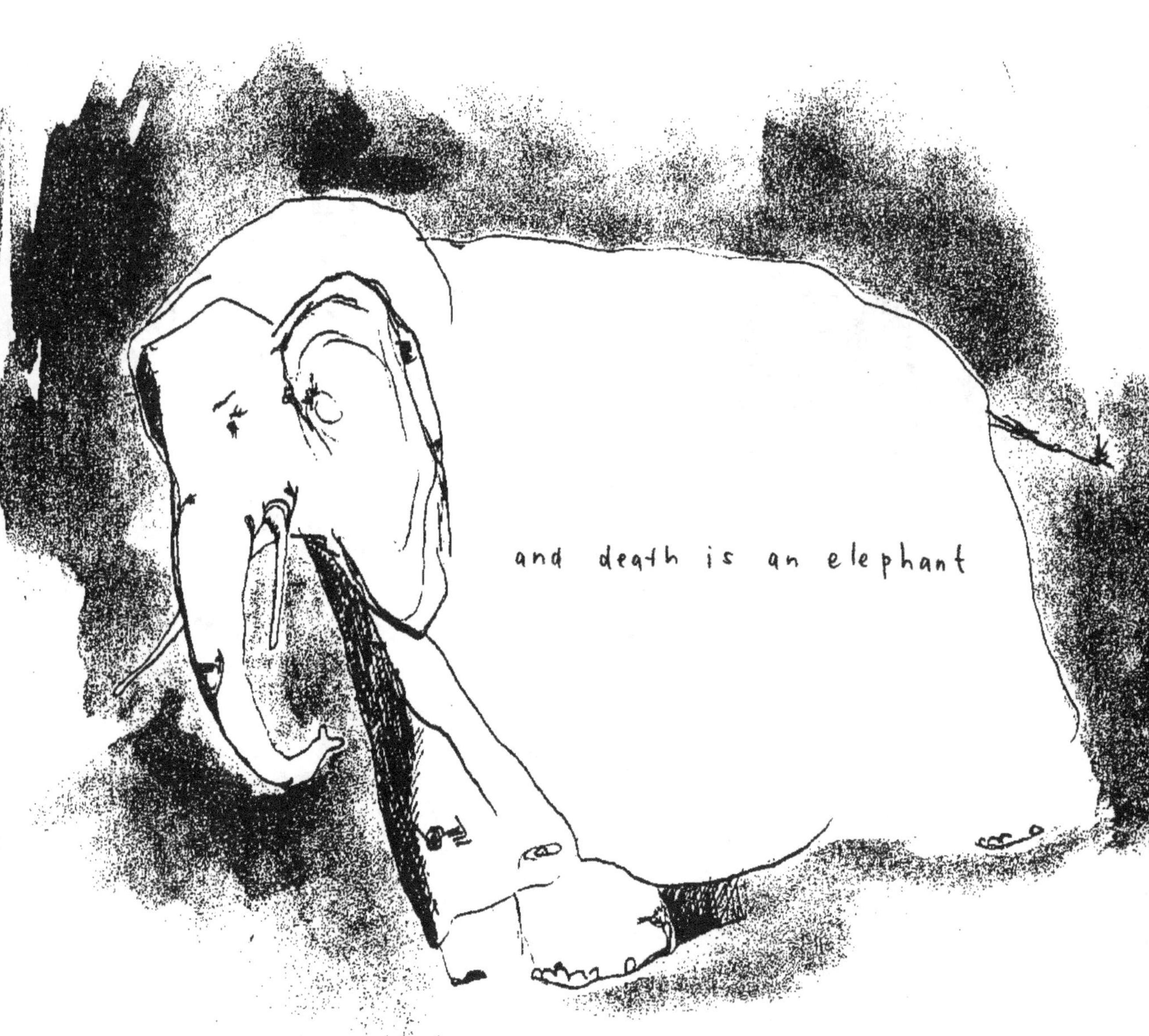
and death is an elephant

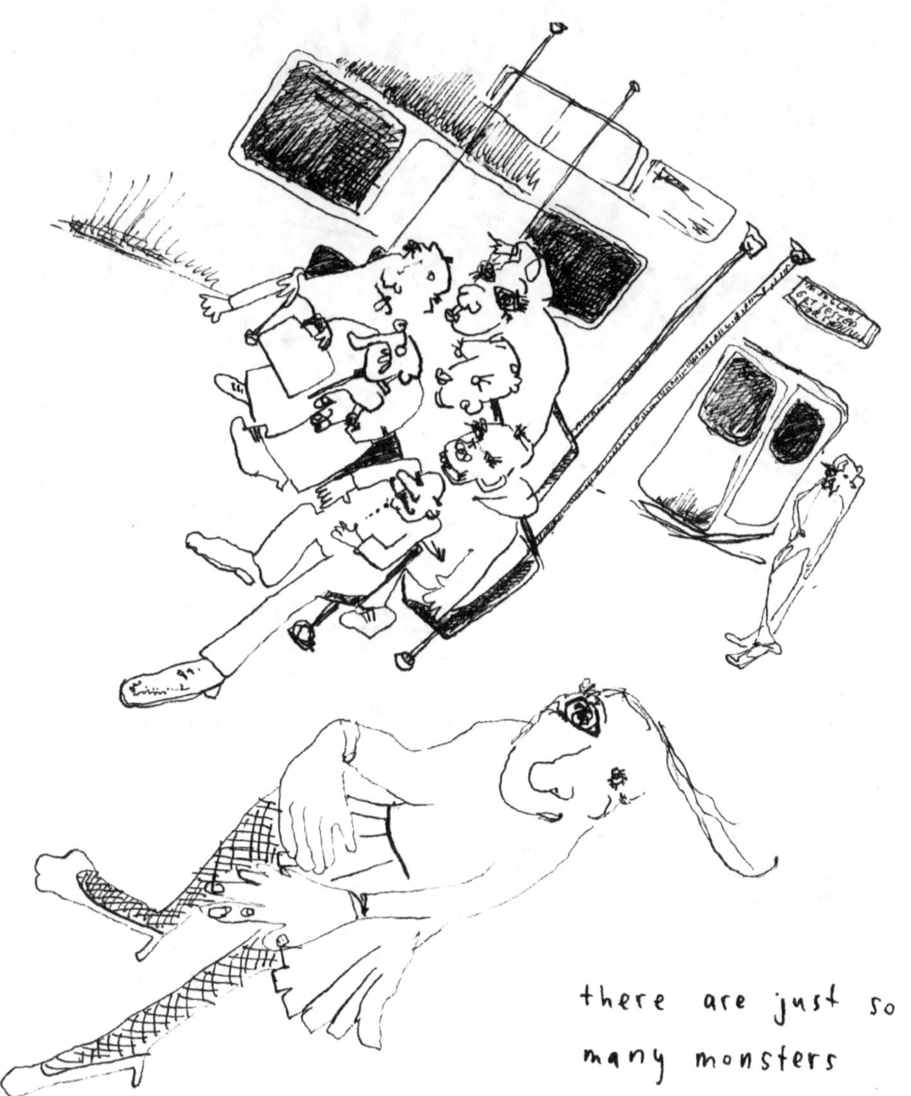
there are just so
many monsters

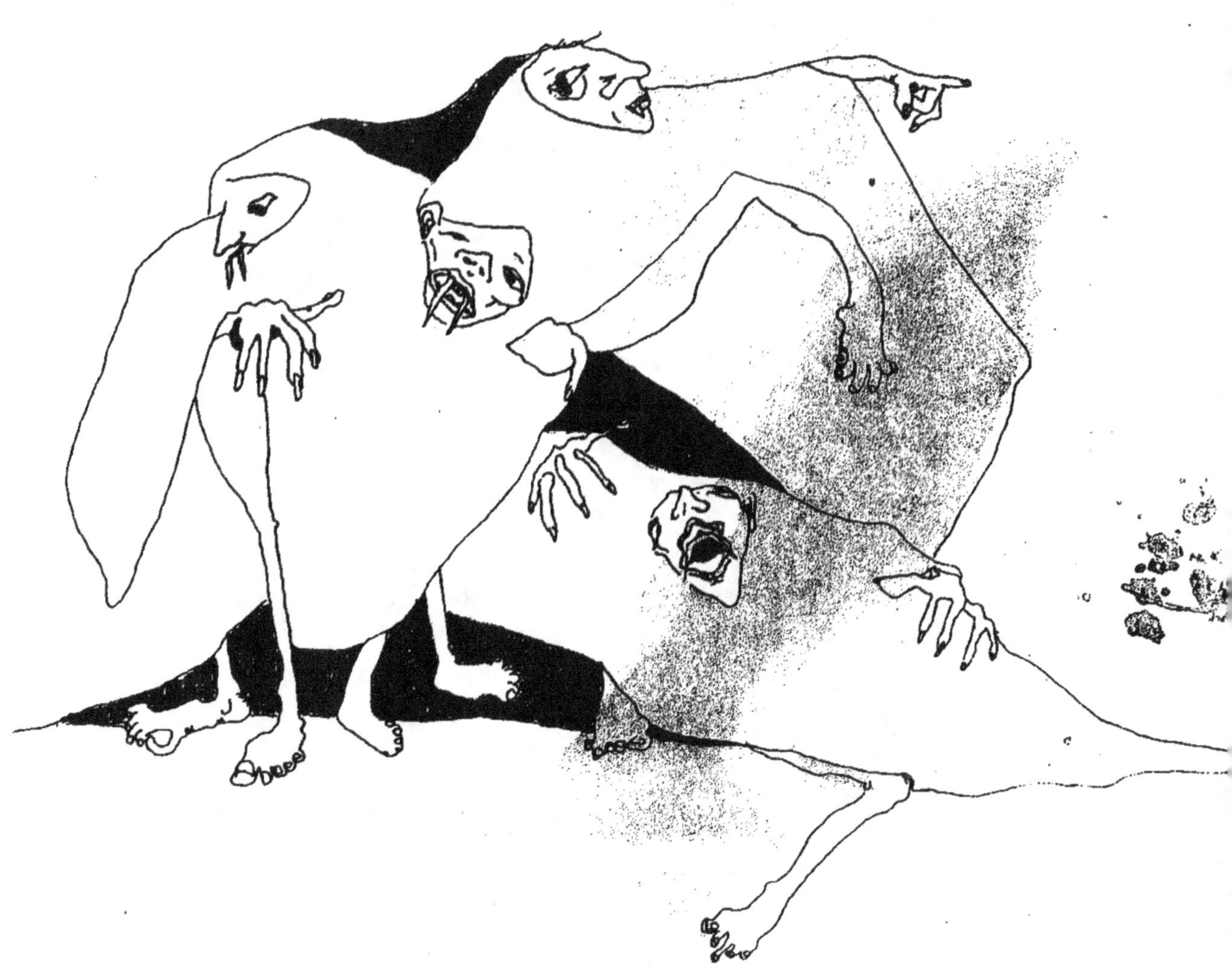

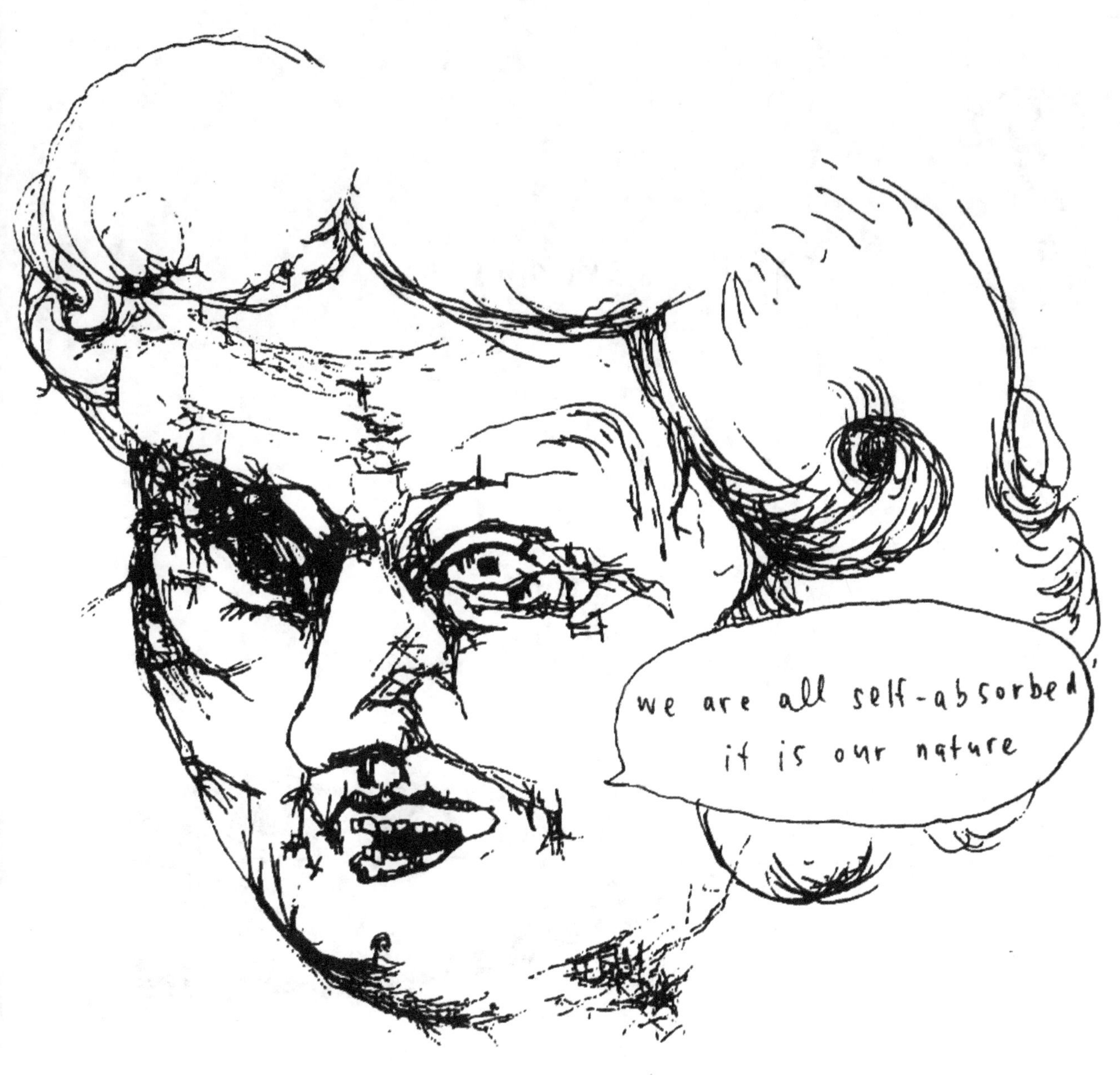
we are all self-absorbed
it is our nature

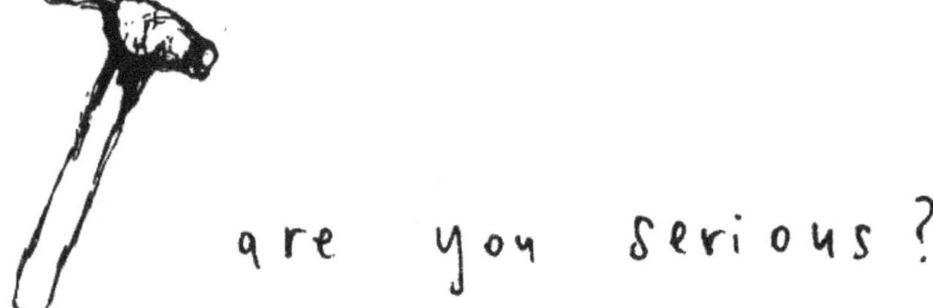
are you serious?

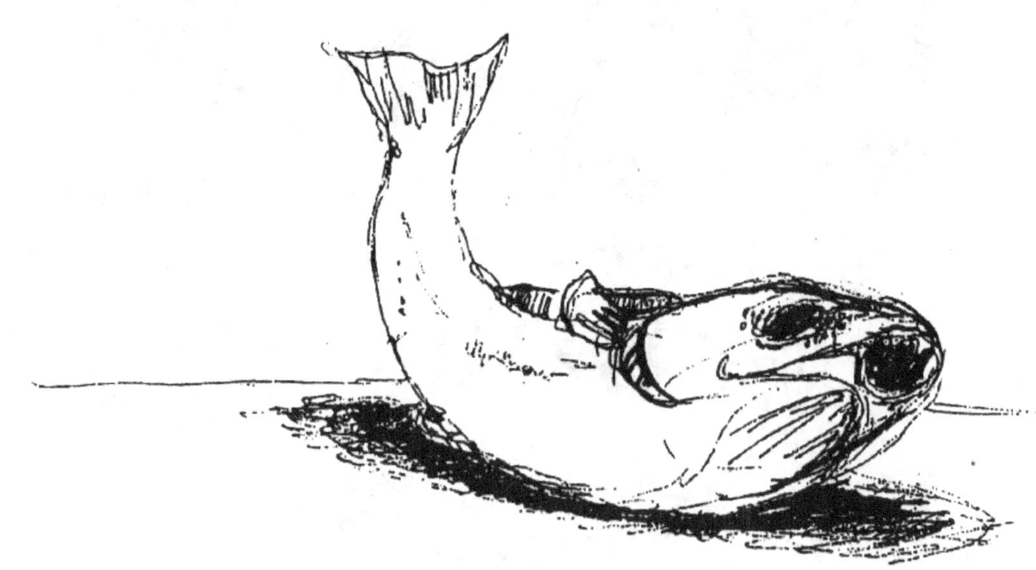

INTERVIEW
WITH COCO PICARD

This is an excerpt of a longer work. Could you tell us a bit about the larger work?

There are sixty-eight drawings total. It starts with a tombstone that says QED and ends with a pig nursing piglets. Between that, there are comics about miracle cures, ingrown toes, singing birds, two sirens contesting their respective authenticity, a minotaur—that sort of thing.

How would you describe your aesthetic?

I'm not sure overall, but *Strategies of Being* is a particular body of work. It was also my first comic. And I didn't know I was making a comic when I made these drawings. There was something very fast about them—they were fast to make, and I think the messy line quality is related to that, too. It's also the first and only time (so far) that I've ever used a fountain pen to draw comics.

Did you have a difficult time deciding on whether to add a title to your work?

No. Not this time. Sometimes I do, but in this case the title emerged with the images. The images and the title felt automatic, almost. When making this comic, it felt like I was living with a feeling that conveyed itself through one-liners that occurred to me over the course of a day or night or week. Each page in the comic is about coping—it could be called *Strategies for Coping*, maybe—but 'being' felt more true to the feeling.

When did you create *Strategies of Being: Illustrations for an Unwritten Essay*?

2005. I originally made it as a handbound artist book with a telegram on the cover. I'd sent the telegram from one address to myself at another address... I think telegrams became obsolete shortly thereafter. I wish that I'd had more opportunities to send telegrams in my lifetime.

What was the hardest part of crafting the piece?

Focusing on the feeling that brought me to it—sort of like sustaining eye contact with something unpredictable.

What inspired this comic? Tell us more about the origins of its creation and whether any aspects of it were inspired by real life.

I was thinking a lot about the loss and determination of human experience. I had big plans to write an essay about that but every time I tried, I thought of pictures and punchlines instead. I made the drawings because I thought they would help me write the essay, but after so many drawings, I abandoned the essay project altogether. The drawings are intended to work as stand-alone, one-off cartoons that slowly build and, taken together, describe the negative space of a non-existent essay.

Tell us a little more about the drafting process. What was the hardest part of crafting this comic?

Aside from never getting to the essay I meant to write, the process of this comic was surprisingly smooth. I usually edit compulsively and for a long time. Most of my comics and novels take years to complete and most of the effort is editing. *Strategies of Being* is unique in that I didn't edit it at all. The drawings came fast and fluid.

I made three times as many drawings that weren't included in the final comic, but the selection process was more like curating than editing. There was a certain point when the images stopped coming to mind. I stopped making comics in (or with) this voice. And then the book was finished. I think I went back to add two or three more panels, but you can tell those ones. The line quality of those looks visibly different.

What instruments did you use here?

A fountain pen and whatever paper was around. There's one comic in the full book that has a smudge of water color.

What other comic mediums do you work in? Do you have a particular preference?

I use micron pens mostly. I like smooth papers but am not particularly picky except that different papers absorb ink differently, so I'll often adjust the size of my pen nib accordingly—anywhere from .05 to .2. Sometimes I use a light table or a backlit window if I am tracing something.

What are the strategies of being?

I like imagining that this could refer to the way a tree grows in relation to its environment—one comic is just a picture of a cypress pine because I love the dramatic way they grow on rocky, windswept coastlines—as much as a figure's relationship to substance or a couple balancing on a unicycle.

You have a wonderful line art stye that feels entropic and purposeful at the same time. Tell us a little bit about the evolution of your style, how you came to it, and what you are working on now.

Wow, I hope so! I really hope that's the voice of the comic—this kind of frustrated line that moves in and out of being articulate or intentional… My other comics are comparatively more crisp. I'm working on a new graphic novel—one with some panels, some mod 60s patterns, some B-movie camp, but the whole thing's still black and white. A black and white, time travel train heist, apocalypse comic with a giant octopus super villain and a space cat.

Do you ever work in color? What are the advantages / disadvantages of working monochromatically?

One of my favorite things about comics is how deceptively humble they are. Pictures make text generally welcoming, I think. And there is something so straightforward about pen and ink—if it's black and white, it's cheap and easy to reproduce and I find something disarming in that no-frills baseline. I think that already sets up an interesting relationship with a reader… Having a monochromatic line drawing is also a way of keeping the line of a given drawing center stage. Maybe in this case, because these panels are all about the ways in which habits are constructed and maintained, it's useful to keep the structure (or the line) visible at all times. Also some of my favorite comics artists work in black and white—Kazuo Umezu, Alan Alagbé, Tillie Walden, Jessica Campbell, Marjane Satrapi, and Keiji Nakazawa to name a few.

Where can our readers find more of your work? Have you been published before?

I have a graphic novel out from *Radiator Comics* called *The Chronicles of Fortune.* The drawing style is related but cleaner. It was written as a series of minicomics that became the novel… I don't think I would have set out to write a graphic novel otherwise. But there was something infinitely more manageable and fun about conceiving and making minicomics. The story follows Edith-May and Fortuna, her superhero alter ego. Fortuna is supposed to be the best superhero in the world, but she suffers from ennui and is useless as a result. She has a bunch of friends—a crocodile, a moth, a goldfish, a mountain, an oven—and they have antiheroic miniadventures. I also have a novella, *The Healing Circle,* coming out in the spring of 2022 via *Red Hen Press.*

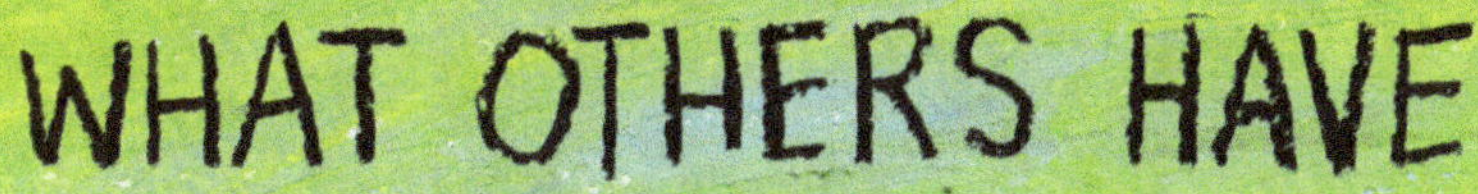

A COMIC BY
LAILA MILEVSKI

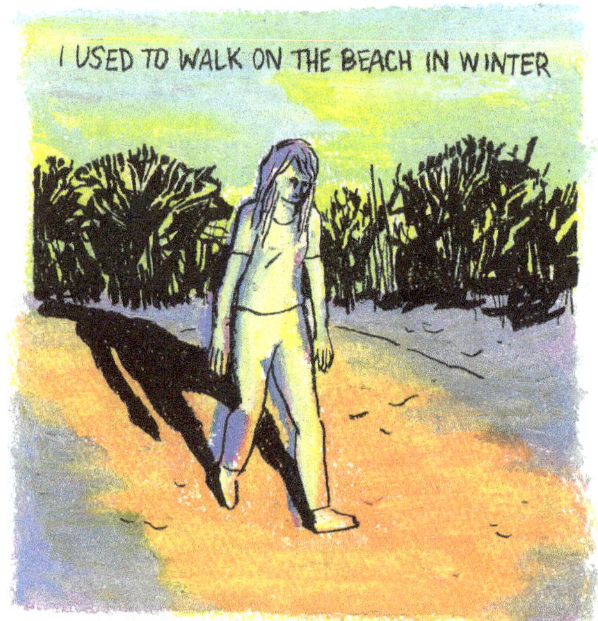
I USED TO WALK ON THE BEACH IN WINTER
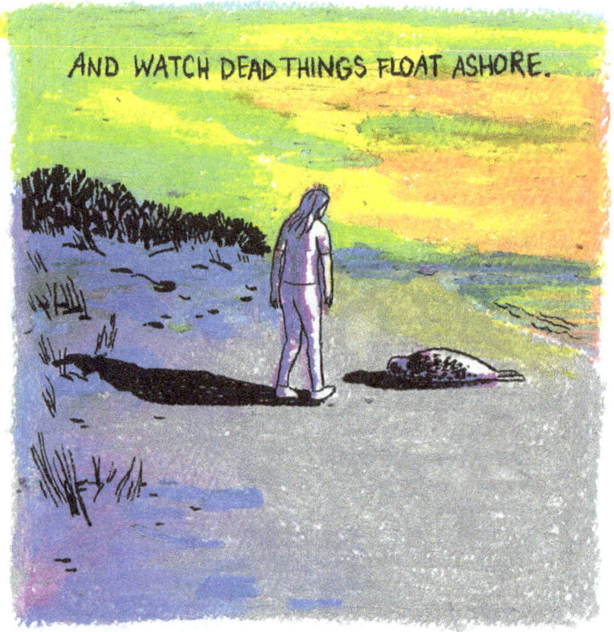
AND WATCH DEAD THINGS FLOAT ASHORE.
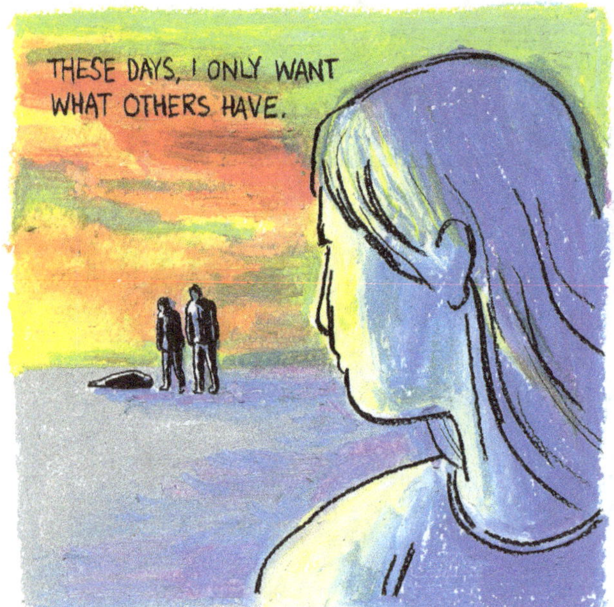
THESE DAYS, I ONLY WANT
WHAT OTHERS HAVE.
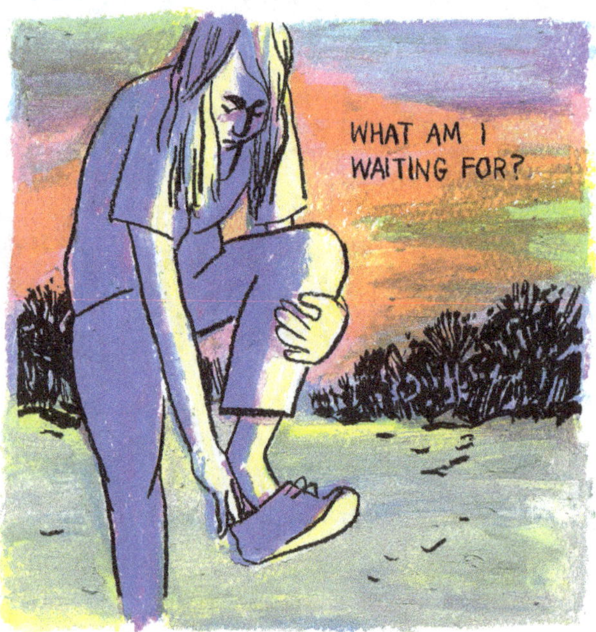
WHAT AM I
WAITING FOR?

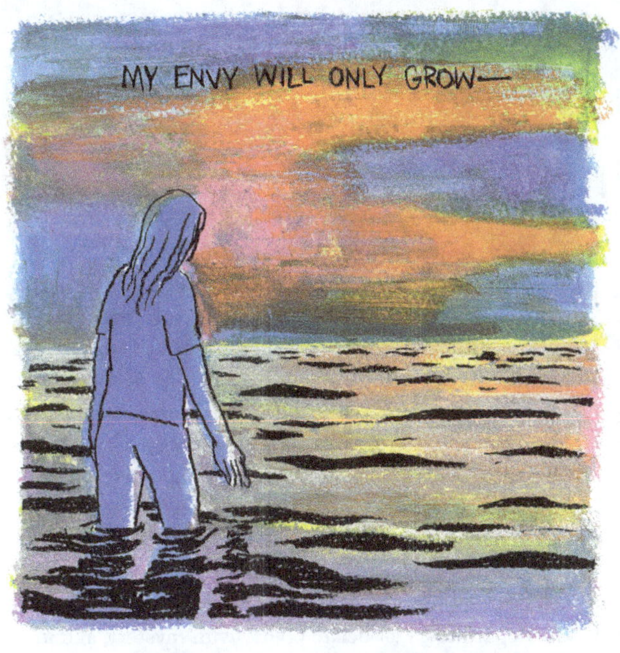
MY ENVY WILL ONLY GROW—
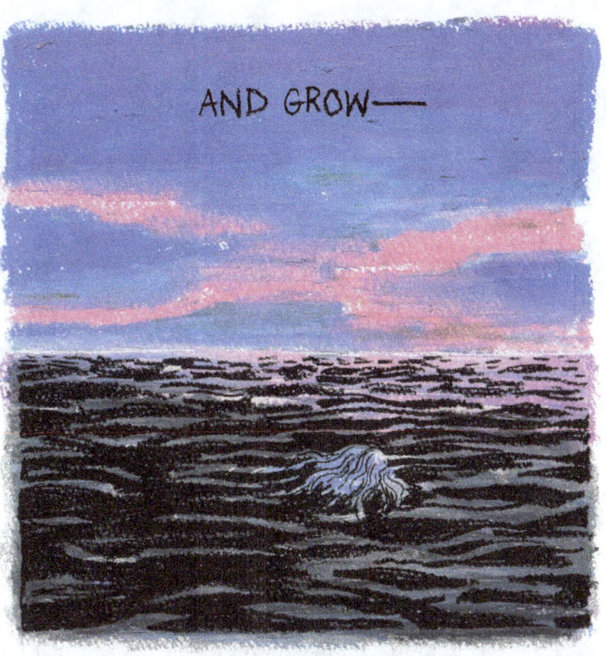
AND GROW—
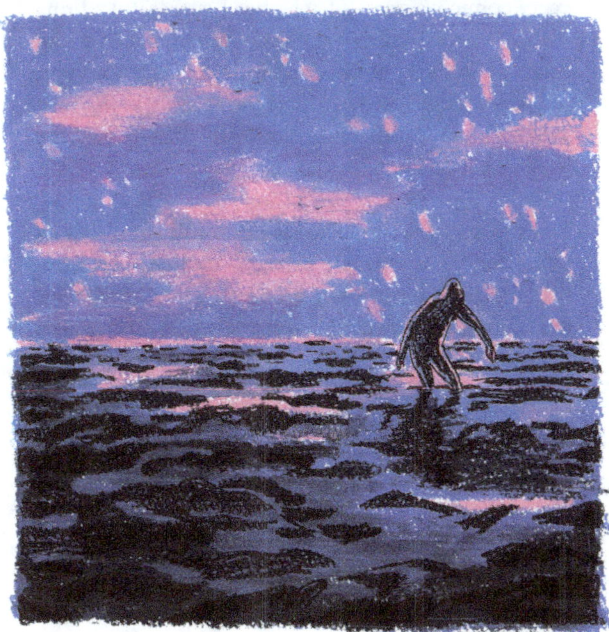
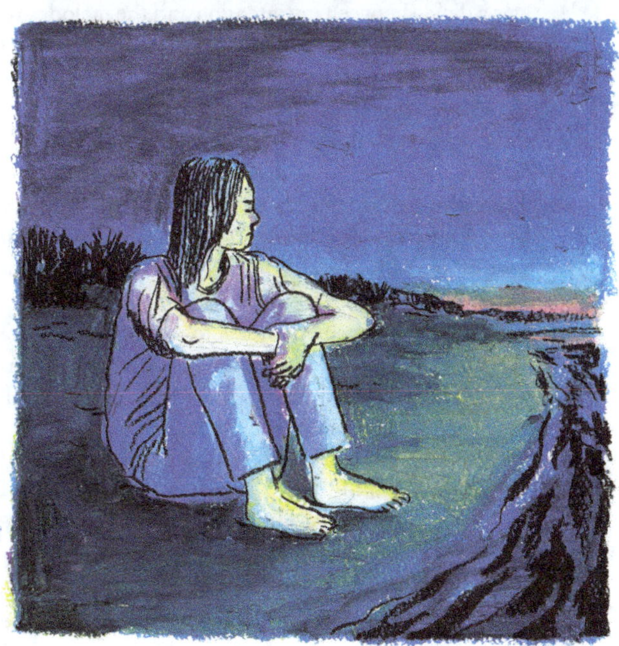

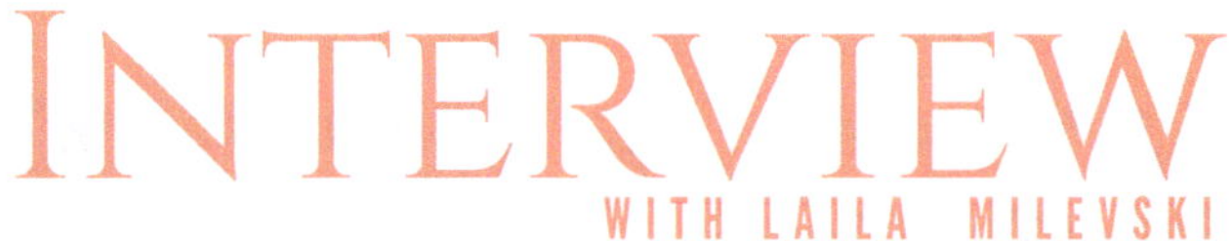

Interview

with Laila Milevski

Did you have a difficult time deciding on whether to add a title to your work?

Yes, I find it difficult to choose titles for most of my work. Too often I choose something from the comic text, a banal but potentially alluring phrase, or, in the case of my nonfiction, a descriptive title/subtitle that introduces the content. In this case it was option #1.

What was the hardest part of crafting the piece?

Developing the end of the comic so it did not veer into dark territory. My characters perform emotions in more emphatic ways than I do, and that creates a divide between my intention and the melodrama or darkness the reader might perceive. I didn't want this to become a comic about self-harm, and I had to change the ending to avoid that, even after feeling that the piece was complete.

The color palette here is striking. Could you talk a little about how you landed on these colors? What sort of consideration goes into choosing a color palette?

I had been pushing myself to use brighter, more saturated, and more varied colors. This comic continued that exploration when I picked up a box of oil pastels. I saw the opportunity to manifest the character's envy and self-reproach through a grotesque and sickly set of colors. The palette also serves the narrative function of showing time passing. The end of the day, its suggestion of rest, contrasts with the fear that this consuming emotion will grow unchecked. Choosing sunset as the setting for the piece may be another way that my creative decisions skewed toward the dramatic.

There's a nice use of the dash on the final page. There are so few words in this piece that each word and punctuation mark take on more responsibility. Could you speak a bit about how you landed on the minimal wording in this piece?

Thank you for appreciating that dash. Lately I've been interested in comics as poetic texts, and so far this has manifested in this minimalism. Poetry is so imagistic, but since the comic is visual, I consider the drawings the source of that imagery. As a result I don't add as much descriptive language within my texts. Sometimes this approach works better than others. Regardless, I associate poetry with mystery, and in every comic it's a test of whether I successfully bring in that mystery without shutting out the reader. As an educator I'm very attuned to image-text relationships, but when it comes to applying those ideas to my own work, it's more difficult to notice the differences between intention and impact.

The main character's face is often fully or partially obscured. Was this a conscious choice, or something that came out more organically? Moreover, what were your preliminary goals in drafting this character?

No, I hadn't noticed it. I wanted to present a detached viewpoint from the character, something like self-observation, though that governed my choices of composition more than my decisions about depicting the face. Maybe this is a visual expression of shame about my own envy. It could be an attempt to show a character struggling with an outsized force in their life—so intense and powerful it feels separate and domineering, even though it is their own emotion and ultimately they are responsible for recognizing and processing it. This comic drew from my emotional experience of the pandemic as well as memories from my teenage years, when I also struggled with emotions I could not name nor express to others. So the character is a conglomeration of myself, simplified and generalized through the drawing process.

Transitioning from creating artwork to fully-fledged comics can often feel daunting for artists. Do you have any tips for aspiring comic writers? What were things you wish you would have known when you were starting out?

This applies for any illustrative endeavor: remember to stick to the feeling or the thing that initially drove you to pick up the pencil and start the project. I've received the most meaningful responses to work that came out of my obsessions and that, in whatever way they could, stayed true to those driving forces, no matter how niche or specific those narratives were. Staying true to the driving force might manifest in the writing or in the drawing, how it is done. I think this last point is really important for illustrators and comic artists who are just starting out and feel the pressures of existing markets and trends when they decide how to make their own work. I wouldn't recommend the haphazard approach that I've taken over ten years to explore my "style," as it's called in the business, but I think it's okay to make decisions about how you draw that honor what the story needs, rather than conforming to what is already out there and is popular.

Where can our readers find more of your work?

Some of my older comics are floating around on the internet (such as on the Comics Workbook blog) and as zines; I've been in a couple of *š* anthologies, published by *Kuš*, a Latvian independent comics publisher. This year I will be working as an illustration and visual journalism fellow at *ProPublica,* so readers should be able to see my work there. I can't say I'm the best at keeping my website or social media up to date, but readers can find me on Instagram (@lailamilevski) and online (lailamilevski.com).

Contributors

Chad Szalkowski-Ference received an MFA from Carlow University. He's currently enrolled in a PhD program at Duquesne University. His work has appeared recently in *Fjords Review* and *Red Earth Review*. He lives with his partner and their child in Pittsburgh, where he adjuncts at a community college.

Mike Nees lives and works in Atlantic City. He is a case manager for people living with HIV and the proud host of Atlantic City's Story Slam series. He studied literature and sociology in the New Jersey Pine Barrens, obtaining his BA from Stockton University. His fiction appears in *The Baltimore Review, Typehouse Literary Magazine, Cleaver Magazine, matchbook, Heavy Feather Review,* and elsewhere. You can find links to more of his stories on his website (storyslamac.com/nees).

Leigh Lucas recently won the 2020 AWP's Kurt Brown Prize for an emerging poet. She holds an MFA in Creative Writing from Warren Wilson and a BA in English-Creative Writing from Stanford. She was a panelist at the 2019 AWP Conference session "Give a Good Reading" and was a finalist for The Los Gatos-Listowel Poetry Contest and the Urmy/Hardy Poetry Prize. Her poems appear and are forthcoming in *Leon Literary Review, The Tusculum Review, sPARKLE & bLINK, A Women's Thing, Jokes Review,* and others. Links to her published work can be found on her website (leighlucas.com).

Heidi Seaborn is the author of *[PANK]* 2020 Poetry Award winner *An Insomniac's Slumber Party with Marilyn Monroe* (2021), *Give a Girl Chaos* (*C&R Press/ Mastodon Books,* 2019) and the 2020 Comstock Prize Chapbook, *Bite Marks*, as well as chapbooks, *Finding My Way Home* and *Once a Diva.* Since Heidi started writing in 2016, she's won or been shortlisted for over two dozen awards. Her work has recently appeared in *American Poetry Journal, Beloit Poetry Journal, Copper Nickel, The Cortland Review, The Greensboro Review, The Missouri Review, The Slowdown with Tracy K. Smith, Tinderbox Poetry Journal,* and elsewhere. She is Executive Editor of *The Adroit Journal* and holds an MFA in Poetry from NYU. You can find her on the web (heidiseabornpoet.com).

Rachel Marie Patterson is the co-founder and editor of *Radar Poetry.* She holds an MFA from UNC Greensboro. Her work appears in *Cimarron Review, Harpur Palate, Pretty Owl Poetry, Forklift Ohio, The Journal, Thrush, Parcel Magazine, Smartish Pace,* and other journals. The winner of an Academy of American Poets Prize, her poems have also been nominated for Best New Poets, the Pushcart Prize, and Best of the Net. Her collection *Tall Grass with Violence* is forthcoming from *FutureCycle Press.*

Samantha DeFlitch is the author of *Confluence* (*Broadstone Books,* 2021). Her work has appeared or is forthcoming in *Colorado Review, The Missouri Review, Appalachian Review,* and *On the Seawall,* among others, and she is the 2018 recipient of the Dick Shea Award for Poetry. She completed her MFA at the University of New Hampshire, where she is currently the Associate Director of the Connors Writing Center. She lives in New Hampshire with her corgi dog, Moose.

Blair Benjamin's previous work has appeared or is forthcoming in *The Threepenny Review, Atticus Review, Bluestem Magazine, Lumina, Spillway, Sugar House Review, Sweet Tree Review,* and *Typehouse*, among others.

The poem in *Driftwood* is one of an ongoing series in which the titles are all fragments of sacred scripture from various faiths. He is the Director of the Studios at MASS MoCA residency program for artists and writers in North Adams, Massachusetts.

SUSAN BRUCE has an MFA in acting. For many years she performed on and off Broadway and wrote poems on the side. She studied poetry at The New School with Kathleen Ossip, Patricia Carlin, and David Lehman. She has a chapbook, *Body of Water* (*Finishing Line Press*), and her poems have been published by *Loves Executive Order, Arcturus, Washington Square Press, Finery, Luna Luna, Yes Yes Poetry, SWWIM* and *805 Lit & Art*. Susan hails from Brooklyn where she also raised her sons. She also surfs and swims as much as she can.

TAYLOR CRAYTON is a twenty-year-old New Orleans native currently pursuing a Bachelor's degree in Psychology from Tuskegee University. She began writing at the age of six, slowly growing up to fall in love with the craft. Her poetry often portrays how Black women navigate through life experiences involving grief, loss, or heartbreak. After graduating from Tuskegee University, Taylor plans to pursue a Doctorate in Psychology.

ANNA LEIGH KNOWLES is the author of *Conditions of The Wounded* (*Wisconsin Poetry Series*, 2021). Her work appears in *Blackbird, Indiana Review, Memorious, The Missouri Review Online, Poetry Northwest, RHINO, storySouth, Hunger Mountain, Sou'wester, Thrush Poetry Journal,* and *Tin House Online*. A recipient of an Illinois Arts Council Agency Award, she has also received scholarships from the Appalachian Writers' Workshop, Bear River Writers' Workshop, and the San Miguel de Allende Writers' Conference. She holds an MFA from Southern Illinois University-Carbondale and a BA from University of Colorado-Denver.

TESSA LIVINGSTONE was born in Long Beach, CA. Her poems have appeared in *Northwest Review, Salt Hill, Juked, Water~Stone Review, Blue Earth Review, Five:2:One Magazine, South Dakota Review, Whiskey Island Magazine,* and *Portland Review*, among others. She holds an MFA from Portland State University.

MOLLY STURDEVANT's writing appears or is forthcoming in *Orion, Newfound, X-R-A-Y Lit Mag, The Great Lakes Review, The Westchester Review, The Nashville Review, The Fourth River,* and elsewhere. She was a finalist for the Montana Prize in Fiction 2019 and a Pushcart nominee in 2020. She lives in the Midwest.

ALLISON BLEVINS is the author of the chapbooks *Susurration* (*Blue Lyra Press*, 2019), *Letters to Joan* (*Lithic Press*, 2019), and *A Season for Speaking* (*Seven Kitchens Press*, 2019). She is the Director of *Small Harbor Publishing* and the Executive Editor at the *museum of americana*. Her work has appeared in such journals as *Mid-American Review, the minnesota review, Raleigh Review,* and *Sinister Wisdom*. She lives in Missouri with her spouse and three children where she co-organizes the Downtown Poetry reading series. You can visit her on her website (allisonblevins.com).

KELSEY M. EVANS is a young artist and designer from Salt Lake City. She is inspired by the natural world and surrounds herself with plants, music, and animals. Kelsey likes to combine color and create texture in her work as a way to express emotion, movement, and spirit. In the past, Kelsey has illustrated multiple books including a series used to teach women's health with the non-profit group Healthy Am I. She is drawn to projects that focus on making the world better and hopes to continue creating designs and illustrations for meaningful causes. Find her on Instagram (@kelseymariestudio) or at a local artisan market around Austin, TX.

RACHEL SINGEL is an Associate Professor at the University of Louisville. Rachel grew up on a small farm in Charlottesville, Virginia. She received a Bachelor of Arts from the University of Virginia in 2009 and a Masters of Fine Arts in Printmaking from the University of Iowa in 2013. Rachel has participated in residencies at the Penland School of Crafts, the Venice Printmaking Studio, Internazionale di Grafica Venezia, Art Print Residence in Barcelona, Spain, and

Wharepuke Print Studios in New Zealand. She has studied non-toxic printmaking at the Grafisk Eksperimentarium studio in Andalusia and will continue her research at Proyecto'ace, an Artist-in-Residence Program in Buenos Aires, Argentina in Summer 2022. Her work has been exhibited nationally and internationally and represented in private, public, and museum collections.

DUSTIN JACOBUS is a Belgian illustrator and designer, with special interests in biomimicry, sustainable design, and futurism. His art-research project Universitas integrates these themes into a futuristic world in which a fictional researcher explores eight solarpunk cities. Jacobus graduated with a master's degree in engineering with a specialization in industrial design. He started his career as a technical illustrator and 3D CAD designer. An overview of his work can be found on his website (dustinjacobus.com).

LIA BARSOTTI HILTZ is a Canadian artist living in Germany. Deeply concerned with health and with human rights, her art and sequential artworks follow the experiences and intimate lives of contemporary career women, living life in the No-Man's-Land between workday deadlines and biological clocks. She is also the creator of *Berlin Tiergarten-Süd: a comics discovery.* A former fiction editor for *Scrivener Creative Review*, Lia graduated from the Etobicoke School of the Arts visual arts program in Toronto and the University of Windsor Creative Writing Masters degree program.

COCO PICARD is a cartoonist, writer, and curator based out of New Mexico. Her first graphic novel, *The Chronicles of Fortune,* was published by *Radiator Comics* in 2017. Her short fiction and comics have been published by *Hyperallergic, The Paris Review, Everyday Genius, Tupelo Quarterly,* and *Wigleaf,* among others. Her novella, *The Healing Circle*, is forthcoming from *Red Hen Press* in 2022.

LAILA MILEVSKI is a comic artist, illustrator, and educator in Baltimore, MD. A recipient of the 2020-2021 Scripps-Howard Visual Journalism Fellowship at *ProPublica*, her work focuses on personal narrative and research-based graphic nonfiction. She has taught at Maryland Institute College of Art and Towson University and tends to a garden of native plants.

www.ingramcontent.com/pod-product-compliance
Lightning Source LLC
Chambersburg PA
CBHW080522030726
47592CB00012B/3433

* 9 7 8 1 9 4 9 0 6 5 1 2 1 *